How to Create
Your Own
High-Paying Job

How to Create Your Own High-Paying Job

37 Tips for Reaching Your Career Goals

Dr. Gary S. Goodman

MEDIA

MEDIA

Published 2019 by Gildan Media LLC
aka G&D Media
www.GandDmedia.com

Front Cover design by David Rheinhardt of Pyrographx

Interior design by Meghan Day Healey of Story Horse, LLC

Library of Congress Cataloging-in-Publication Data is available upon request

ISBN: 978-1-7225-0216-4

10   9   8   7   6   5   4   3   2   1

Contents

Introduction
& Overview

Are you unemployed? Or, are you overworked, underpaid, and stuck in a lifeless job, reporting to someone who doesn't seem to be doing much better than you are? You are not alone. Corporations once needed large inflows of middle managers and the formally educated. Many of these posts have disappeared or have been displaced by outsourcing, offshoring, international competition, and by technology.

There is a widespread and growing under-employment problem facing almost every society. Many are working at jobs that do not require the experience and schooling they possess. In the United States up to 44% are under-employed; in Canada this number is 40%.

Though there has been some job growth over the past few years, these jobs are mostly lower-paid without a solid ladder to success. In this original and groundbreaking book you'll learn how to develop your own highly compensated career opportunities.

Specifically, you'll learn new and exciting ways to:

- Identify your marketable skills and attributes.
- Translate your strengths into in-demand occupational titles.

- Express your capabilities in results that are highly sought after by today's organizations.
- Market yourself in several ways: As an employee, consultant, coach, vendor, and contract associate.
- Get paid what you're worth, and far more through enhanced negotiation skills.
- Develop new, highly paid occupational titles that put you into a class by yourself.
- Learn to overcome the hurdles and barriers of the traditional job market.
- Use advertised job listings as springboards to better jobs.
- Reach top executives presenting yourself and your capabilities at the highest possible levels, and more.

First, let's put today's job challenges and opportunities into perspective. Visiting a relative in the hospital I found myself drained and in dire need of food. I ambled over to the cafeteria, a cheerful place with nice employees. Then I saw something hugely disappointing. The food was practically nonexistent. There were three pieces of pizza in the carousel, some rice and beans, and a twist or two of purplish mystery meat. I vibed the guy in front of me to leave the pepperoni slice alone; it was mine! I was so hungry I didn't care about the meager offerings. I ate what was there.

This is the job market in a nutshell. It is a cafeteria without any food you really want to eat. What it does offer is short on flavor and nutrition, and it does not sustain life and limb. You pine for the real thing. But you are so starved that you are willing to settle for jobs as they are presented.

Imagine an alternate reality. You stroll into a fancy big-city restaurant. It is elegant inside and the waitpersons are all attentive and respectful. You study the menu but don't see anything that you desire. So, you say to the server, "I'm sure your chef is very capable. Would you please ask him or her to make something special for me, from scratch, not from the menu? I'm up for anything tasty, but I do especially like seafood, pasta, and well done vegetables. I'm sure the result will be very satisfying. These were almost my exact words to a server in Chicago on one of my business trips. The result was a magnificent, fresh meal, and an utter surprise and delight, to me, to the server, and to the chef.

This is the way the job market can be and the way it actually is for people that know how to navigate it properly. You are not settling for crumbs or for stale leftovers. Everything is fresh, interesting, and surprising. Savvy people are having "off-the-menu" experiences all the time, while the mass of humanity is praying the last piece of petrified pepperoni will be there by the time they reach the end of the line.

This book will show you how to evolve from grubbing to fine dining. You will learn how to create your own high-paying job, a job that will be in keeping with your skills and desires as well as financially rewarding. When you realize that you can call the shots and "order a job" that will fit your exact tastes, you will rise to the top of the food chain and never see the world of work in the same way.

I've done this, repeatedly over the course of my career, and you can, too. One way to do this is to package yourself as a consultant. Let me share with you some of the biggest secrets that management consultants know that you probably don't know. I've been a management consultant for decades and I have also been an employee at both large and small companies. The differences are many and significant.

Consultants are not conventional job hunters, though they are constantly on the prowl for paydays. They may look at classified job ads not as desired positions that they can fill with their labor. They see ads as indications of change, of growth at a given company. To consultants, employment ads are signs that there are bigger and better possibilities in store at those firms. Ads say, "We need help! We can't do everything by ourselves or with our current staff."

That is a powerful admission. It is the opposite of what you find at smug companies in recessionary times, where they staff the barricades to keep job-marauders out. It has been said the "The wise person creates more opportunities than he is handed." Smart consultants can keep themselves busy with one assignment after another, especially at larger firms that can see their value. So, if they are kept busy and are pretty much always on the payroll, who cares if they are not called "permanent employees?"

That term, permanent employee, is an oxymoron, a contradiction. If the last decade or two have shown anything conclusively, it is the fact that companies shed employees, continuously, and without guilt. No one is truly permanent, including the Chief Executive Officer.

I don't say this to make you cynical or anti-corporate. I point it out to clear up any misunderstandings you might have about the best relationships to form with them. Having an assigned space in the parking lot and an employee badge may feel comforting and give you a sense of routine. But being paid the bigger bucks is more important than these trivial symbols and satisfactions. I don't care what people call me, providing I am paid and I am paid well!

For the better part of two years I did a consulting project in Houston, Texas. One contract led to the next, and I found it was more convenient and it actually saved the company money for me to live at the Four Seasons Hotel, renting an apartment-suite by the month. At one point, I was the fourth highest paid person at the firm. Because the company was publically owned, this fact had to be disclosed in its periodic Securities and Exchange Commission filings. This unexpected visibility put pressure on the corporate officers to hire me as an employee. The firm offered a serious six-figure salary, which was less than what I was pulling down as a consultant.

I declined, partly because I felt I could earn more and retain my independence by not coming aboard. Plus, I had a much better lifestyle being a "temp." I commuted from Los Angeles and almost 100% of my expenses were paid. Today, I would not care. For whatever reason, if a firm needs to put me on the payroll as an employee, and the opportunity is lucrative enough, I'll go with the flow and consent to it.

Note that it is common to morph from being a temp to being hired "permanently" if you start as a consultant. If that is a goal for you, fine, but you may want to disguise it. Starting as a consultant is one way to create your own high paying job because you are in charge of its design, especially if you bring your idea to the firm. The fact that you design the work, its location(s) and hours, is huge and can be a major financial benefit in itself. I'll detail this advantage, later.

Consultants look at companies and see problems that need to be fixed. The more valuable the problem, the more value you can get for solving it! Most employees, who are not senior managers, are not paid to spot these problems or to focus on remedying them. Employees are paid to do what is in their position descriptions. They are also handed miscellaneous tasks that their supervisors deem important at the time. Employees, in other words, are hired and paid to execute routines, rule-governed, repetitious tasks. What you need to appreciate is this. If your job can be reduced to a routine, it can be performed by anyone. Then, that worker can be replaced by a bit of software or by a robot.

High cash-value jobs are not routine. Let me give you a personal example of a non-routine opportunity that eventuated in my doing lots of high paying consulting gigs.

I was an Assistant Professor at a leafy Midwestern University. For many with my academic training, it would have been a dreamy assignment. It was full-time, permanent, and it could have lasted a lifetime, because the post was on a tenure-track. But I wasn't thrilled with it. I had earned twice as much money, eight years and three college degrees earlier, when I worked in the private sector for Time-Life. At the university, suddenly I had to prepare for and teach four different classes each semester, work during winters, co-coach the debate team, and run the annual honors conference, lining-up dignitaries to participate.

I was a great teacher (and still am!). My evaluations were always stellar, and I had a terrific time speaking before groups. "Why don't the best teachers earn a bundle?" I muttered to myself. "Shouldn't they make as much as other highly trained and competent professionals?" I decided to resign from my post.

What I ended up doing was creating my own high-paying job. Within 18 months, that job would pay me more than ten-times what I was earning as a professor! Here's the good part. I still taught through universities, so my credentials weren't wasted in the least. But I wasn't tied down to one campus. I taught at 35 universities, simultaneously.

I invented my own subject matter. These courses attracted the largest business book publisher in the world: Prentice-Hall/Simon & Schuster. They invited me to write a book. Within five years I published six titles with them, many of which became bestsellers. Later, I would need to redeploy my assets again, creating a high-paying job as a consultant.

I'm going to detail for you the mechanics of spotting opportunities, creating your own job, and then selling it to a company, to a school, or to a nonprofit organization. I will share with you the exact way that you go about "creating value" as your number one focus. Let me give you a closer glimpse of this now.

Sometimes I ask participants in my "Best Practices In Negotiation" seminars to tell me how much they would gladly pay me if I promised to earn them two million dollars. "Would you pay me 10% of that, $200,000.00?" I ask. Everyone nods, enthusiastically.

"How about 20%; $400,000? Would that fly?" Most are still nodding, some less vigorously.

"What if I asked for half, for one million bucks; would that be okay?" A few participants are still in the hunt, knowing they'll earn a million for themselves.

I continue the questioning; whittling back the amount they receive until they look puzzled. At that point they start challenging the value of my proposal. Somewhere after I descend below the 50% point, they perceive the proposition as inequitable, as unfair to them. I have to remind them, "Look, before I came along you weren't going to earn anything like what I'm offering, so why not take 20%, $200,000.00, and be happy with it?"

Having quickly gone from earning 90% of the proceeds and then being urged to accept a mere 10% flips their value meters. Instead of focusing on their gains, on the fact that they are still ahead and what they are receiving is a windfall, they count my money, instead.

Their goal changes from sharing to preventing me from achieving what seems to be a lopsided gain. This example stands for many things, but for the purpose of showing you how to create your own high-paying job, it signifies this crucial proposition:

You can charge what you want for your talents and labor as long as you deliver enough perceived value to someone else.

Let me turn this example in a different direction. Let's say I promise to deliver $2 million of value, but I will only charge minimum wage to do it? That would seem totally out of synch, correct? You would quickly doubt my ability to deliver, my sincerity, and perhaps my sanity. Nobody "gives away" that sort of value for something so trivial, correct?

If you are going to offer big value, every reasonable person believes you are entitled to get big value in return. Unless, that is, you are called an "employee." If I hire you as a minimum wage worker and you come to me with a way to save or earn two million bucks, I'll take your idea, cash it in for its full value, and I may overlook even giving you credit for the idea, let alone paying a bonus or a serious percentage of its value.

Companies believe they own *everything* employees think and do and invent while they are on the job. This is the Mephistophelean pact we make when we seek the security and steady pay of typical jobs. Companies willingly pay what they feel they must pay, and nothing more. It is the rare employer that purposely overpays industry averages. If they do, they see a bigger picture.

Henry Ford, the automotive entrepreneur, famously inaugurated "The Five-Dollar Day" for his assembly line workers. At the time the prevailing pay for similar work was only one-dollar. Ford's fellow captains of industry excoriated him for his largesse. He would make their wages look depressed, by comparison.

Ford realized if he offered five bucks he could have his pick of the best workers in America. He was correct. They flocked to him from far and wide to fill his jobs. He also knew he was producing a product that needed purchasers. On $5 a day, Ford's employees could live decently and afford to buy a car.

Recently, a company in the financial industry in the Northwest "Pulled a Ford" and decided to pay its workers at least $70,000.00 per year. Its competitors also wailed, feeling the boss was a traitor to his class. But the publicity and goodwill the firm achieved outweighed the minuses.

Again, these are rare examples. Being gladly "overpaid" is unlikely if you are an employee, by designation. My point is you should work at your greatest level of contribution and earn a fair proportion of the value that you confer. How you label your contributions is crucial in justifying higher income. When I discuss the $2 million example I offered above with my seminar attendees, I am speaking from actual experience. I was charging by the day for my corporate seminars and consulting in the areas of selling and customer service. In doing so, I was limited by how much I could "reasonably" ask for six or eight hours of classroom time.

There were hundreds if not tens of thousands of decent speakers that would gladly provide similar services for what I was charging, or less. This "invisible hand" of potential competition depressed my wages as long as what people believed they were buying was generic "training. But then I created something astonishing. It was a conversational device, a talking-path for customer service reps that would enable them to make phone calls 20-30 percent shorter, but better. If a call center had 100 employees, they could suddenly handle the workflow of a 120-seat center, with no added investment in plant and equipment and labor. At an imputed cost-per-seat of $100,000.00 per year, I was able to save 200-seat centers $2 million in the first year, alone. A full time "trainer" on a company's payroll might earn $40,000 to $60,000 per year to conduct seminars. A consultant whose emphasis is training might pull down twice that amount. But someone like me, illuminating an entirely different path to profit via labor savings, could be paid a lot more of that expected $2 million worth of first year value. I could easily earn $500,000 and up, couldn't I? That's just the fee for *one* client! I defined value in a way other consultants and on-staff employees did not. Though it is common to measure average call length, these functionaries didn't know how to abbreviate conversations while making them better. Like the saying, "Everyone complains about the weather, but no one does anything about it!" the challenge is known, but the remedy isn't. That is, until I come along.

Let's pause for a moment to delve more deeply into that age-old question: What's in a name, especially an occupational title? For instance, being a "trainer" is a decent job as far as jobs go. But if you permit yourself to be defined as a trainer, then you will probably top-out in earnings at a fairly low level. It is essential to define yourself differently, in a way that the job market doesn't already have a low-value "peg" for.

It is a fact of life that companies will define your contribution at the lowest possible level they can get away with. The more your responsibility sounds generic, something anyone can do, the better. If you are an author, someone that writes original articles and books and other potentially high value products, that is one thing. But in the hands of position description hacks, you will be called at best, a "writer," but more frequently these days, a "content provider."

Content is like an empty pail: very plain, made of cheap metal. As a "content provider" you might be paid minimum wage or slightly higher. On top of this, you'll be expected to work quickly and relentlessly, spitting out lots of content under strict, supervised deadlines. Taking charge of your occupational title is happening frequently these days. I mentioned a title that has been around for many decades: CEO or Chief Executive Officer. Along with the President, this is pretty much the top dog at a company. This title spawned another that was typically adopted by what was known as the company's Controller. Some years ago, Controller morphed into Chief Financial Officer, CFO. A bigger, more prestigious title sooner or later justifies earning bigger and more prestigious pay.

This is the main incentive people have for creating better job titles. Plus, and this is crucial, for a time there is no widespread standard of comparison available. Someone in Human Resources cannot easily learn what CFOs earn if there are very few CFOs to which one can compare. This is why right now there is a proliferation of "Chief" titles in corporate America. Vice Presidents and Senior VPs of Sales now seek the title, "Chief Sales Officer." Heads of PR departments are re-branding themselves as "Chief Communication Officers." This list is growing. Some of the justification for seeking a larger title is that there has definitely been job enlargement in companies, especially since the Great Recession. Jobs have been eliminated but also merged, so people are wearing several hats while doing double and triple-duty, often without more pay.

Where you look for high-paying opportunities is very important. Going to sectors where there seem to be lots of jobs is enticing. But it is also where you will find the lowest wages and the most competitors. For example, right now, if you search for sales jobs in Los Angeles, you will find two types with more listings than others. Jobs are aplenty in solar energy and in merchant credit card processing. I can tell you with utter certainty that these fields are super-saturated. The big money in them may have existed two to five years ago, but by now, the meal they're serving is old, cold, and pre-chewed.

You need to apply some creativity to develop high-paying opportunities for yourself. In the movie, "Pan's Labyrinth," a girl takes a piece of chalk and draws a door on her wall. She opens it, and enters a lavish and amply stocked banquet hall. Some people find the idea of drawing a door where there is none impossible, silly, or useless. Walls are walls and doors are doors. Along with the majority of other job seekers, you may believe every business has a front door, and that's where you need to enter. If you don't use that portal, you will never get in.

There is only one flaw in that scenario. It is the belief that if you use the same old door everyone else uses, you'll gain admittance. That is not reality. Most candidates are trying to stampede through one tiny opening, typically, for one tiny job. I say if you want to find true treasures, and unexpected pleasures, you should draw your own door. Those that do are greeted with banquets instead of crumbs.

I am going to teach you how to open bigger and better doors. Specifically, you will learn how to reach the top ranks of companies. You'll begin your quest for a higher paying opportunity by getting through to top officers in corporations and other organizations. These are people with the power to hire you and more. They can custom-design a position just for you, if they are impressed enough with the value you are offering.

Here's an example: I spotted a dynamic, growing education company in the classified ads the other day. Obviously, they're scaling-up their operations and from what I could detect, they are profitable. I'm sure they can use my consulting services. Now let's imagine what is happening. Because of their ad, they are being pummeled with applications, from what I would be told later, thousands of them. This is like a huge crowd that is trying to fit through the eye of a needle. If you are interested in the posted opportunity (which I am not) good luck creating meaningful differentiation between yourself and the hordes of competing resumes. But what if you could draw a door, an alternative way of introducing yourself, a portal that may be completely inviting and potentially unguarded? You can enter this door when you wish and get a real human being with influence and decision-making power to hear about your credentials and desirability. Better yet, what if this person whose attention you are getting is the head honcho, the president of the firm? That person could invite you to send your resume directly to him or her, and in turn, she would pass it along to the staffer doing the hiring. Topping that, the president might create a special, new position, just for you. What would your chances be then, of getting noticed, eliciting a meaningful interview, and developing a highly paid relationship? You'd jump to the head of the class, wouldn't you?

This is what I recommend to people that I mentor. Don't go where there is a crowd and try to stand out among zillions of competitors, or lookalikes. Go where there is no crowd and where there is no competition. The ad for that educational company indicated an outsourced entity was doing the hiring. I checked out that firm and realized communicating with them was a fruitless waste of my time. With a little research, I found the name of the president of the company, his location, and his phone number. I called. After selecting a promising voice prompt I was put through to an extension.

"This is Ron," the voice said from the speakerphone. Same name as the president, I thought. It was the president! I went on to pitch him. During that chat I got his personal email address and I gave him enough information about me to let him know he was speaking to a force of nature. He said some interesting things, such as "Normally I don't answer the phone," to which I replied, "The more I call, the luckier I get." I mentioned I am the bestselling author of *Reach Out & Sell Someone* and *You Can Sell Anything by Telephone*.

Now picture this. I am asserting I am a genuine expert and he needs me. And I am proving the point by breaking the rules, getting him on the phone and having a twenty-minute, meaningful conversation with him. He got a real-time demo proving I practice what I teach. He will never forget the call and the fact that I made my point. I differentiated myself.

Everything I do with him from this point will be seen as peer-to-peer, because I reached out and sold him on my significance. I am not an applicant or supplicant.

It's okay to apply for jobs the conventional way. But keep in mind how unlikely it is that you will (1) Get in; (2) Stand out; and (3) Earn exceptional pay. Later on in this book, I'll share winning scripts and specific techniques you can use to reliably get your information in front of the right people, right away. I simply can't wait to share the essential details involved in creating your own high-paying job. And it really is just that: a creative process that is interesting, adventurous, exciting, and lucrative.

This book will help you to take charge of your life-style and your life. In the 37 tips that follow, you will find motivation and a specific set of practices to reach your career goals. We've already made a solid start. Let's move forward, onward, and upward!

Tip 1:
Create a Parallel Career Track

I worked my way through college and grad schools. It wasn't easy, learning full time and working full time. But it yielded some extraordinary benefits that I continue to cash-in today. Let's skip to today and I'll show you what I mean.

In the last week I have: (1) Practiced law; (2) Practiced real estate; (3) Sold a loan; (4) Contracted to write a book and record an audio version; (5) Pitched a corporate training program; (5) Coordinated my teaching assignments at two major universities; and more.

This means I am a lawyer, real estate broker, financial salesperson, negotiator, professional writer, recording artist, corporate consultant, and college professor. Each of these capacities brings income to me. Some of them are well paid. Worked together, they are even more rewarding.

When I was a freshman in college, my Sociology professor, Dr. Quinn, predicted each of us attending class that day would have a minimum of four careers during our lives. That sounded daunting and exhausting. Yet, I've engaged in seven or eight careers, depending on how we count, during the last week, alone! Surely, these jobs require various amounts of study and preparation, lasting years. But they are not sequential, as we think careers must be. They are simultaneous. This is a form of multitasking that you should consider doing, as well. The first step is to be open to taking on different career identities. You cannot become so inflexible that you tell yourself, borrowing from my trades, that because you are a professor, selling is beneath you. Start instead with the premise that all honest work is worthwhile and meritorious.

If you enjoy doing a job and it helps you to earn a living, that's good enough. You do not want to get ego-invested in believing you must be a specialist in any one area to respect yourself or be respected. Specialization has been keenly pursued in developed societies ever since the industrial revolution. Learning to do one small thing and to do that well has been seen as a ticket to success. And it worked that way, until recently. Let's look at just one of my specializations, practicing law.

As I communicate this to you, some say there are far too many practicing attorneys in the State of California, at 225,000, way more than the market can handle. Of that number, about 170,000 are engaged in legal work while the rest are in different occupations. An oversupply of lawyers means wages become depressed, jobs in the law are harder to find, and if you want to create a high-paying occupation for yourself, choosing to do it through a legal practice may not be the best way.

That is, if *all* you do is practice law. It so happens in California you can sit for the real estate broker's exam if you have earned a law degree from an accredited school. Naturally, you need to take a broker preparation course. But if you have the brains to be a lawyer, believe me, you also have the smarts to be a realtor. I've had both sales and broker licenses. The latter enables me to do more things and to earn higher commissions.

Most people practice real estate part time, as salespeople. They buy and sell for their own portfolios, saving on commissions, or they do some transactions for their friends and families or both. Generally this is an accepted practice, though uni-career types that believe you should do only one thing at a time might gripe about it. The fact is if you simply do one real estate deal each year you will spike your overall income significantly. For this reason, I would urge you to get a real estate sales license, which is easy and inexpensive to do. You do not have to be a lawyer for that, and you can save yourself money even if all you do is buy a property for yourself every so many years. Once more, my point is that having lots of arrows in your professional quiver and actually shooting them off together can make a lot of sense. To mix the metaphor, it is akin to having your fingers in lots of pies.

Now let's turn to some of the skills that are shared in common by the career paths that I am pursuing simultaneously. I honed my selling abilities when I worked for Time-Life. I became their top seller and then a sales manager while I was a full-time undergraduate student. This single skill has been worth a tremendous amount of money to me. As I mentioned a moment ago, in the last week I did some successful selling. In fact, I'm almost always selling. I do it to get universities to offer my classes. In some cases, those initial sales last for a decade or more. Once my courses succeed, typically I'm asked to do more teaching at those schools. Likewise, I need to sell my books and media programs to publishers. At times, I do this directly. And at others, I have an agent that places my projects. To get an agent, you have to sell the person on your earning power and creative capabilities. Then, you have to sell the person on the value of each new project as you conceptualize it.

Consulting for a living involves ceaseless selling and self-promotion. Typically, projects only last for a while and one needs to be quickly followed by another. To keep your calendar full, you need to keep hustling, and this means selling. To create a high-paying job you will need selling skills, as well. You might be thinking, "But I don't want to be a salesperson!" Yup, I know the feeling, and I have to overcome it practically every day!

Selling gets more lucrative, more routine with time, but it always requires a certain amount of effort. Read my book, *Selling Is So Easy, It's Hard*. It will help you to avoid the 77 predictable pitfalls we all fall into.

For now, let me urge you to appreciate that we're all salespeople, butcher, baker or candlestick maker. And the first sale if you want to earn high-income is between your own ears. You need to sell yourself on your own value.

Tip 2:
Take A Tip From Steve Jobs

Steve Jobs, co-founder of Apple, was trying to build an electronic device when he was in his late teens. Only problem, he did not have the money to buy the parts required. Then he had this brainstorm. David Packard, then the hugely successful founder of nearby Hewlett-Packard, probably had those parts. Jobs looked up Packard's home phone number. It was in the book! The teenager explained his project and asked if the honcho had some spare parts.

Packard did better that that. He was so impressed with the moxie Jobs showed in phoning him, that Packard gave Jobs a summer gig assembling the same devices that Jobs wanted to build on his own. You can read a million things into this story. For our purpose, though, I hope you will take inspiration from it.

To his credit, Jobs thought through who was likely to have the parts he wanted. But there is something even more significant here. Jobs started at the top. His first call was to the boss, someone who could make *anything* happen. If someone in a firm can donate spare parts to a kid, it would be the owner of that firm, correct? Plus, and I've seen this time and again, if a leader is impressed with you, they will make a spot for you. They will put you to work somewhere in their organization. This way, they can learn about you. What kind of worker are you? Punctual? Tardy? Creative? Dedicated?

They may not give you the keys to the kingdom, at least not right away. But they will let you prove yourself. And if the boss is mentoring you, even behind the scenes, believe me; you will be on a fast track, even if you start in the mail room or in front of a machine on the factory floor.

This brings me to a point. Most of us, when we're opportunity hunting, waste our time trying to impress the wrong people. Let's say you do what most job seekers do. You spiff up your resume, buffing it to a high gloss. Then you send it off to the Human Resources department at a company. And you wait for a reply. None comes, and you wonder why? For one thing, HR people don't create jobs out of thin air. Their workday does not consist of sifting through resumes, finding interesting people, and then making customized jobs for them.

They receive requests from various parts of the firm. The sales manager says she needs two more account executives. Would HR please recruit them either by placing ads or retaining personnel agencies to identify suitable candidates? Or, that sales manager says she needs a sales assistant to help with various things. Then, HR might write a position description, or take an existing one pertaining to an Executive Assistant, change a few responsibilities and buzz words here and there, and then advertise that job opening.

Let's hark back to David Packard. After Steve Jobs called him, the boss might have asked his HR people what tasks they had that related to the gizmo Jobs was trying to build. Voila! They found an assembly job doing exactly what Jobs wanted to do. But let's say they didn't. Packard could have easily said, "Well, I'd like to try this kid out, somewhere. He sounds like he has a decent technical mind and he can build things. What have we got?"

Remember, this is the founder and owner of the firm asking HR to find *some spot*, maybe *any spot* to put Jobs to work. You know that HR individual will come up with *something*, correct? What I'm saying here is that HR people are *reactive*, not proactive. They respond to needs that others have identified. They don't roam the corridors breathlessly inventing things for people to do, and especially innovating tasks. That is above their pay grade.

Now that I've used that cliché, let's examine it further. Typically, HR folks don't control the purse. I see this all the time as a speaker and consultant. For example, a company came to me asking about one of my negotiation seminars. The head of HR made the initial inquiry. What would it cost to bring my training to that firm? Immediately, I inquired about the amount of funding they had budgeted. They didn't have a budget. Well, this is par for the course, I thought. Someone, who is a line manager, perhaps the head of sales, wants the training. But he or she delegated the recruitment task to HR for the purpose of doing some initial "shopping" and tire kicking. Of course, after I quoted my fees, the HR fellow got sticker shock. It was so far above his pay grade that he had no context to evaluate the value associated with the price I quoted.

I have *never* sold my consulting services directly to an HR person or department. They are not the buyers, and if they think they are, believe me, what they permit you ask a fee or a wage will be depressed. At some stage you may have to deal with these generally nice folks, if only to complete paperwork associated with your job or gig. And they may have some influence over hiring decisions, again, at some stage.

But they are not the real buyers. The real buyers are folks that are higher on the food chain. Steve Jobs intuited this fact. That's what gave him the motivation to make his first call to David Packard. You need to go to the top, as well. Look at it this way. If you shoot for the moon and you miss, you still might end up in the stars.

I've contacted company presidents and owners and they have referred me to their inferiors. However, the clout of having a top dog say to an underling, "Hey, see if this person has something to offer us," is implicitly a hint that they believe you have something to offer! Why would the most important person at the firm bother to pass along my name if he or she wasn't convinced I had at least some potential value? If you contact HR instead as your opening gambit, even if they like you it is highly dubious that they will send your name upstream to more important folks. Why is this so? It is risky for them to take a chance on doing anything outside of their standard routines and responsibilities.

Let's say that hypothetical boss passes my name along and the underling thinks I'm a waste of time; that I have nothing meaningful to offer. Will the boss be at risk for having made the referral? Of course, not; bosses are secure in that way. They can say, try this or that, with impunity.

Let's review what Steve Jobs did, which got David Packard to create a job for him. Jobs thought through who would have the components he needed, in other words, he identified the company that was probably building devices of the type he wanted to build. The principle he followed is this: Don't visit a nearby palm tree if you're seeking oranges. Palms may grow dates and possibly coconuts, but oranges just won't fall from them.

Identify the type of company that is doing what you want to do. Next, develop a short pitch. Jobs said he was building something and he thought Packard might provide him with some parts. I'm inferring this was approximately the gist of the conversation. Your pitch doesn't need to be fancy. We'll invest more time in constructing your pitch later.

Jobs got Packard's phone number. It was in the phone directory. Don't assume every step of the process will be difficult. With a minimum amount of digging or a few phone calls, you can get to nearly anyone's communication doorstep. Jobs made the call to Packard! For some folks, lifting the teeny phone to make such a call can feel as onerous as lifting a 2,000 ton weight. Later, we will talk a bit about phone fear, who gets it, and how to overcome it.

Finally, Jobs was open to any offer Packard made. And he seized the opportunity Packard handed him. Without that summer gig, there may have been no

Apple, and no Steve-Jobs-the-Legend. But as you know, Jobs created that job at Hewlett-Packard. He didn't see an ad for it. And he didn't waste time with HR folks. He went to the top, and not too long after that, the top went to him—the top post, that is.

Tip 3:
If At First You Don't Succeed,
Try Something Else!

We are creatures of reinforcement, plain and simple. This means, if we do something that ends well, we are inclined to repeat the behaviors that preceded the happy outcome. For example, let's say you found a good summer job by going door to door in the retail district of your small town where you happened upon a Help Wanted sign. The people inside were warm and courteous and supportive. You were hired on the spot and time flew. You earned a decent piece of change, for a kid.

Based on that one experience, you might expect your next opportunity to come the same way. Easily, without any muss or fuss, you believe good situations will practically fall into your lap. This is a more favorable outlook than expecting the job hunt to be hard and filled with obstacles. If you're dreading it, you might procrastinate and fail to do even perfunctory employment seeking behaviors.

This is akin to what I have experienced at numerous sales jobs. As part of an extended interview process, I have been put on the phone with a minimum of training. A name or two along with phone numbers have been supplied to me. I have been expected to "reach out and sell someone" which happens to be the title of my best-selling book.

Here's what happens. At those jobs that work out well, almost invariably I have been the beneficiary of beginner's luck. Much more often than not, I have made a sale on my very first try! At one place, an office supply wholesaler, I phoned a baker, as in butcher, baker, candlestick maker. My goal was to sell him a gross of ballpoint pens—that's twelve dozen writing instruments, 144 in all. I followed the presentation, word for word, doing my best to bring it to life. And at the end of it, the baker did his part; he bought! As I recall, I earned about $35.00 for that first conversation, which wasn't bad money at all for a graduate student. The owner and sales manager were shocked, in a good way, of course. The sales manager exclaimed, "He's a master, a master!" which was high praise, indeed.

And I went on to prove them right. I became the undisputed champion seller of ballpoint pens to customers in the food service industry. I focused mainly on selling to restaurants, which no one had really mastered, before. I joked that you could navigate your way across country by car, stopping along the way only at restaurants I had sold, and never go hungry! It turned out to be a great part-time job for me, enabling me to pay for a new sports car that was the envy of my fellow grad students, and probably most of my professors, as well.

I sold pens on top of teaching classes at two universities, so I did pretty well for myself. That pen job was a straight commission affair. If I sold I earned, and if not, well, you know. But I never experienced a dry spell. From that first sale onward, I did okay for myself.

The moral to the story is this: Very often, if a job is right for you, you will show a knack for doing it, immediately. The required skills will come easily to you. From a practical standpoint, this means you should be prepared to try many jobs before settling on any one job.

Let's look at the other side of the coin. Let's say what you have chosen to do, or the only job you could find at the time was an utter pain. Every shift is just terrible to do. Possibly, you hate your boss or your work mates or your assignments, or all of the above. That's a bad sign!

I delivered fish and poultry during the hot summer in a truck that wasn't air-conditioned. It was a smelly, greasy, and exhausting dash from one doorstep to another. One day I was called on to bring a case of wine down from the loft. I tripped, fell forward, and twelve bottles broke with a deafening sound. Fortunately, I was unscathed. But there was a message in this mishap. That wasn't a good place for me. Shortly thereafter, the boss got that message, too and fired me. Almost instantly, I got a new and better job that helped me to keep my head above water and pay for my apartment while I was starting college.

Being fired is almost always helpful! It turns a page or closes a chapter for us. Surely, it may seem involuntary and inconvenient, but it is almost always a good thing when viewed from a distance, later on. You don't want to "get good" at something you hate! This may seem ridiculous, at first, but hear me out. You want to do easily and gladly and fruitfully what you are a "natural" at doing.

The problem, or better said, the tragedy, is that people don't find what they are good at doing, easily or quickly. They may even invest a fortune, mortgaging their futures to student loan debts going to law school or into a field someone else wants for them. Then they discover they have no real feeling for that career. In fact, most of the time they are in school or practicing that occupation, they report feeling vaguely "numb." This isn't a version of that rock ballad, "You've lost that loving feeling." They never had it to begin with.

I was in the car leasing business right out of college. On paper, it was a great job. The firm provided me with a brand new car to drive, every three or four months. Imagine that. I was 21, and I could tool about in fantastic rides, one after another. I didn't even have to pay my car insurance. The firm paid that, too. Plus, I earned good money that enabled me to live well. But the stress was incredible. I had some unpleasant physical symptoms, including high blood pressure.

One of my leasing clients was an attorney. I told him I had always dreamed of going to law school. So, generously, he invited me to do a ride-along with him. What we did over the course of the day was file documents downtown at court. I met his office staff. And we ran into one of his clients, a guy that would go on to become the heavyweight-boxing champion of the world.

But there were no courtroom heroics. There was nothing much to see, except coordination and communication. Bob said to me with a knowing smile: "Gary, the law looks glamorous, but a lot of it is just filling out and filing the right papers at the right time." That day was well invested. Some of my illusions were dashed. Later, after I launched my consulting career, I'd complete law school and pass the bar. But my eyes were open and I had other reasons for becoming licensed as a lawyer than being a glorified filing clerk.

To sum up, let me say you should try a lot of things. Put your toe in several streams to see which ones are hospitable and comfortable. If you hate something right away, that's a good cue to leave it. If you feel every day is unrelentingly dull or filled with stress, get out of it. Don't wait to fall from a ladder with a case of wine in your hands. "Love at first try" is a very good sign. I'm so used to it that if I don't succeed right away, I don't "try, try again" as the old adage would have me do. "I try, try" something else as fast as I can!

Tip 4:
Tell Yourself, "I'm Worth It!"

Some years ago a gentleman asked me how much I charge for my consulting services. I quoted my rate, which given my skills and experience, was quite reasonable. He balked and said: "The average consultant in Los Angeles only charges $X per day, I'll have you know." To which I replied, "I'll have you know, I'm not *average*."

I realize this is kind of a cute exchange, a neat little quip, and a clever rejoinder to someone that wants to reduce your fee. But that's not my purpose in sharing it with you. There is a powerful truth in what I said. I am *not* average. And neither are you. However, in today's labor marketplace there is excruciating pressure to yield to the idea that we are the same as everyone else and the only meaningful differentiator is price.

Let me take you on a trip down memory lane. My very first consulting assignment came through the academic department where I taught part-time, at California State University, Northridge. A part of the Los Angeles County Medical Association needed some speech training. After others on my faculty passed, I grabbed the opportunity. I needed the dough, plus this was a great way to transition into the world of paid consulting. Now you should appreciate that I came to LACMA with what is called a "halo" over my head. I was recommended heartily by my department chair. It cost me nothing to sell the group on retaining me. The lead was handed to me on a platter. And I wasn't really competing with anyone else, so when my chair said I was a good fit for that audience, he was credible and believed, right away.

Today, that same group might never seek out the head of an academic department at a university as a means to obtain a suitable candidate. They will Google for names and be deluged with page after page of results from speech consultants, each one with a long list of references. How will searchers differentiate them? They may call a few and ask for quotes, for prices. After receiving them, they'll cycle back to the ones they were impressed with. Then they'll ask them to do the assignment for the lowest fee they were quoted. Effectively, they'll do exactly what that fellow did when he asked what I charged. They will quote an "average" fee back to you, or say it's a readily available price to pay and hope that you'll yield to that.

Given the fact you know there are at least a hundred similarly situated consultants in Los Angeles or in your locale or not far away, you'll probably buckle under to the price the prospect wants to pay. But therein lies doom. As a businessperson, and even as a part-timing moonlighter, you cannot afford to give away your stock in trade, your services. You absolutely must make at least a minimal profit. A profit is essential if you want to stay in business tomorrow and to serve another client.

Do not succumb to selling "price." You must instead sell "value." You are selling the benefits you are giving people for the price they are paying. Essentially, you can't be bashful or insecure. Boldly, and if necessary, brashly, you need to assert, "I'm worth it!" I am using consulting as an example to make my point, but the same idea applies to creating your own high-paying job while justifying being paid superior wages. You need to operate from the belief contained in the adage: "You get what you pay for."

When people pay more, they get more; it is not when they pay less, they get more. You are not Wal-Mart. You don't want to position yourself as offering the "low price, always." Wal-Mart can do this for a variety of reasons, and consumers can actually demand it for a variety of reasons. The first is the fact that a 48-inch television by a certain maker is standardized. It is the exact same appliance in Wal-Mart as it is in other stores.

Human services are always different. Physician "A" may have gone to the same medical school as Physician "B" but the experience you have in dealing with them will be far different, because people are different. Let's look again at the TV purchase. Strictly speaking, while you may purchase the identical TV at Wal-Mart that you would get at COSTCO, you may like the customer service more at one store than the other.

Here is the human factor sneaking back into the equation. The TV may be exactly the same, but the buying experience is different. In this sense, my professor and management guru Peter F. Drucker had it right: he said, "There is no such thing as a commodity." 18 carat gold is 18 carat gold the world over. It is a commodity, in a strict metallurgical sense.

But buying it may be a lot easier at your corner jeweler than it is over the Internet, or vice versa.

Companies that hire you want to make you feel you are a commodity. They pretend there is nothing that distinguishes you from the next person standing in line with a resume. But this is patently false. If it were true, why would they interview you? Why wouldn't they place their labor forces in the poorest nations on earth to reduce their labor costs to the lowest they could possibly be? Some try this and they find there are huge hidden costs in offshoring their business functions. Then they return to their country of origin to fill their labor needs.

So, you are different, but merely asserting this fact isn't sufficient. You cannot get away with saying: "I'm better because I'm better." That is tautology, circular reasoning. You have to state *why* you are better and exactly *how* you are different. And you need to explain how *your difference makes a difference.*

Drucker was running a class at which one of my fellow students, a senior manager at a financial company said, "Our customer service is better because we have lots of local offices for our customers to visit and our main competitor only has three to serve the entire country." Drucker asked this penetrating question: "How do you know your customers want, need, or even appreciate having so many local offices available to them?" The professor pressed his point. "If you were to unbundle those offices and price them separately, would customers pay at least a little more to use them?" In other words, you do differ from your competitors in regard to how many offices you have. But is this a difference that makes a difference to customers, not just to you?

If you want to create a high-paying job for yourself you need to justify getting the high pay. This will require differentiating yourself in a meaningful way from look-alikes, people that say they do what you do but do it for less. In the best case, you will be able to make a claim to 100% Exclusivity. This says, "No one else on earth does what I do."

When I devised a conversational path for customer service reps to use, I was the *first and only* consultant to offer that path. I constructed it, from scratch, embedding into it a word-for-word *script*, assigning definite tones to expressing those words, and outlining the optimal *timing* with which to use that conversational device. It delivered meaningful differentiation: Award-winning service as measured by an outside firm, service that retained customers at a lower cost.

If clients wanted it, they had to get it from *me, and me alone.* That's exclusivity, and it is really saying your product or service is practically 100% different than anyone else's. When you can say this with the authority of results, you are free to fetch a premium price for what you are offering.

The opposite is appearing to be a 100% commodity. Then, the only meaningful differentiator may be price. There are other factors that you can point to. One is convenience. If you're selling your labor, you might be able to start right away. You could be ultra-local, meaning you can arrive at work earlier or stay later without inconvenience to you or to your employer. You could have a great personality! Don't laugh. I retained the same accountant for years partly because he was a great guy. On at least one occasion he cost me about $25,000 in unnecessary taxes, which finally led to our parting of the ways.

If you can assert in a nice way that people say you are a pleasure to work with, this goes far in differentiating you from the next candidate. What I'm saying here is that if at first, it appears you have no meaningful differences that people will pay a premium for, you are wise to look again. You probably do have meaningful differences that people will pay a premium for. I encourage you to try harder, first to see them, and then to argue for them and their value.

Remember: You are not a commodity. You are not "average." If you succumb to these labels and generalizations you will find it hard to justify creating a high-paying job. Instead be prepared to assert, time and again, you should be paid more because "I'm worth it!"

Tip 5:
You Can Get More Than Dog Treats

Woof! More businesses are saying they are dog friendly these days. But that is not a plus if you and your workmates are the dogs. I monitor job listings as part of my career coaching and book authoring activities. Much can be learned from them, spotting the trends they contain.

One type of listing that I have become acutely aware of boasts that the company doing the recruiting has "free snacks" and a "fully-stocked kitchen." What does this really mean? And to whom, exactly, is this sort of perk attractive? If you are a strapping adolescent or the cartoon character, Gaston, from Disney's "*Beauty and The Beast*," then you're hungry all the time. I get this. I have kids. (How else would I know about Gaston from "Beauty and The Beast?")

Is this employer trying to attract famished teenagers? It is possible, that they really do want 18 and 19 year-olds to apply. But if this is not the case, and they're "paying" these folks with popcorn and pizza instead of a plump paycheck, then I'm more than a little concerned. Hooking people on freebies is really a way of playing the shell game, that shady carnival con where a pea is hidden under one of three rapidly shifting half walnut shells. "You put up your money and you take your chances!" the smiling gent in the straw hat says. Quickly, he shows you the pea as it is tucked under a shell. And then his hands whirl three shells together and then apart. You're dizzy from all of the action and you choose one of the shells. No pea! You're wrong! "Care to try again?" he sympathizes.

The company that is dishing out all those dog treats is making you monitor the wrong shell; in this case, the one with crumbs under it instead of a five-course meal. If you are making good, great, or outrageous money somewhere, do you really care if they toss you free peanuts? Of course, you don't. You can have gourmet take-out delivered three times a day, and not blink.

Indeed, if you love where you work, and the primary reason you would love it is that you are successful there; then on-site snacking is the last thing on your mind. If, however, you are working for trifles (instead of truffles) then you need to rationalize why you put up with the paltry pay instead of insisting on receiving more. "Little dog treats" distract you from the fact that you are being terribly taken advantage of. They are stealing thousands from you in genuine pay, but you don't notice because they seem to so generously reward you with $1 lattes.

And by dog treats I don't mean just nibbles and noshes. Dog treats include other silly perks. "Company softball team" is another one. Now, I love baseball and in a pinch, softball is a decent substitute. Heck, if you tell me I can play whiffle-ball and hit it with a little plastic bat, I'm game. But these supposed perks that are designed to create bonding and "team spirit" should be salaried, and be voluntary.

Let's say there is a company ballgame scheduled for Thursday night at 5 or 6. You'll be there until 9 or 10.

Are those extra hours to be donated, by you? If it weren't for the game, would you invest your off-time scrounging up 17 other people to play softball on a Thursday night? Even if they pay for the pizza (Here we go again!) who cares?

Repeatedly, as part of a super-successful sales team I declined to go on paid vacations to Las Vegas on the company's private jet. These trips were touted as rewards for great team performance. Yet, when I added everything up, I'd be out of pocket for transportation to the airport and other incidentals, and I wasn't being paid for my time.

I had better things to do. So, I asked the company to pay me the cash value of the trip, what they would have spent on room and meals, had I attended. I refuse to donate my weekends, any of them, in the name of team building, self-congratulation, and the like. I made the right call. I would have been exhausted when I returned on late Sunday evening. That means I'd be dragging my butt on Monday, a working day where I should have been in top form, making money. So, they were giving on the one hand, but taking on the other. It's that darned shell game all over again!

When companies throw those dog treats around they expect a payback. You need to salivate, bark, roll over, or do some other trick to show your appreciation. All of which is really costly and a very bad bargain to make if you are a job seeker. Let me put it this way. Avoid companies that offer free snacks, a fully stocked kitchen, a company baseball team, free vacations and day trips, a fun atmosphere, a cool culture, and other sizzling treats. There is no serious money to be made there, unless you own the kennel or the company that's stocking the kitchen.

They're appealing to amateurs and not to professionals. They want you to reach for the wrong walnut shell, the one where the pea will never be found.

Money is money, and if you want to create a high-paying job for yourself, don't accept substitutes that compensate you at a fraction of your worth, while getting you to settle for the wrong prizes.

Tip 6:
Think Bigger

I'm going to tell you about the most effective and influential customer satisfaction campaign ever created. I know all about it. I'm the only one who knows all about it because I am at the center of this tale. The story you're about to experience is my story, how I revolutionized customer happiness and loyalty. You are also part of this history because you've been served and satisfied through the communication devices I crafted.

In fact, if you phone nearly any large company for help, you'll be treated to at least a diluted version of my conversational path. I say diluted, watered down, because I haven't directly trained or licensed most of the firms that are now imitating my design. They are doing the best they can with what they have. In this book, you're going to learn far more than they know. And you will probably end up doing my "stuff" far better than they do.

If you walk into a branch of Citibank practically anywhere, and you speak to a teller, you will hear an approximation of the talk-path that I devised. If you call your cable TV or Internet provider, their tech support and service staffers will use my guidelines. At this point, I estimate that my technique has now been used in billions and billions of conversations throughout the world. In the same way McDonald's has served "billions and billions" of customers, I have too, through my model.

As you learn about the development of my methods, you will also come to understand that most businesses are clueless about how to create customer loyalty. They are ignorant because they haven't paid the price to scientifically learn what happy customers do, what they say, and how they behave as transactions come to a conclusion.

I have done these things, and more. Not only have I come to understand happy and loyal customer behavior in the wild, I've learned to tame it. With my methods we can create exceptional results, increase profits, cut costs, reduce personnel, make training easier and more meaningful, measure the right behaviors accurately, motivate and properly compensate employees, and do much more. Specifically, we can cut costs by 25-30% and radically improve customer outcomes. On what authority do I say this?

A Call to Greatness

I was a very successful college professor, but it wasn't enough. I needed to earn more money, and my ambitions wouldn't be satisfied from getting tenure, the only significant monetary incentive my profession offered.

So, I transitioned into consulting, specifically training people from companies in my techniques for selling and serving customers. These methods married my advanced academic training with the corporate experience I had garnered while working full-time as an undergraduate and graduate student.

Initially, I offered seminars to the public through a network of universities I had established. These programs were very well attended, and my income shot up by a factor of 10.

But again, I wasn't satisfied. Were the people that attended my programs actually using my methods back on the job? I needed to know. I phoned them, and while they praised my ideas they weren't so diligent about applying them. This didn't surprise me. As a former sales manager I knew well the tendency to treat techniques like a cafeteria, selectively picking out what appealed, while shunning the most nutritious items.

I transitioned into doing onsite training at companies where I could introduce ideas and through one-to-one coaching, supervise their implementation. Increasingly, my programs became customized. I was called on to address specific problems and opportunities. In this context, I got a call from the CEO of a major financial company. I had successfully trained his mid-six-figure earning sales people a year before.

Now, his challenge was customer service and his question was straightforward: "Can you fix us?" That simple question would be a call to greatness, requiring me to outperform any customer service improvement program ever devised.

From Worst to First

The group I was assigned to "fix" consisted of about one hundred people in Houston and another hundred or so in Kansas City. The service team was in trouble. Out of a field of 26 companies it scored at level 24 in customer satisfaction, as measured by a respected industry research company. It would be an understatement to say their customer mood was not great.

In fairness, this wasn't the fault of the service team alone. The company had not distinguished itself in the investment returns it provided to its clients. Besides the low industry satisfaction rating, there was a more serious indicator that clients were displeased. Assets under management were shrinking; "leaching" as they say in the trade.

With reduced assets under management, the company earned less in fees, and this affected everyone's pay, most notably the CEO's. So, the marching order, "Fix us!" meant what I was about to undertake was much more serious and sensitive than "Please & Thank-You Training" as most customer service instruction is derisively dubbed.

And to this extent, I'd be operating out of my comfort zone. Frankly, much of my income derived from customer service training had been devoted to seminars I had standardized. Top-rated as these programs were, they wouldn't reverse the serious negatives this service cohort faced. I needed a lot more insight into how to create loyalty, which is the opposite of what was happening through the flight of assets. I had to devise techniques so powerful that they would create a halo over the company despite its middle of the road financial performance.

Not easy, but I was given a lot of leeway to figure things out. Within a year of the time I had built my design and rolled it out, that company's service group soared in the ratings, from #24 to #4. Then, in the second year, it moved into the #1 spot and stayed there for 12 years. *The Wall Street Journal* said it well. The company skyrocketed, from "Worst to First."

The more people you help, the more money you can earn. Think bigger, think BILLIONS.

Tip 7:
Think: Who Will Stop Me?

There is only one person holding you back from making progress and that person is you. I know, this sounds like only so much new-age blather, but it is reality. You have to take the governor off of your own achievement. This is especially the case when it comes to earning an exceptional income.

You want a great job, one that will pay you far more than the average. This requires a belief system to support that aspiration. If you are deeply committed to this objective, nothing can stop you from realizing it. But if you are at all ambivalent, or fearful that this is out of reach, then it will be so and remain so.

I was hired to consult by a California-based software company. A middle manager came to one of my public seminars. He liked my ideas and decided to champion them at his firm. This is a quite common sequence. Someone gets a sampling of my techniques, appreciates them and then takes the relationship to the next step. This would become a very good project for me, one that yielded a ton of money in a short period. I was also able to requisition the third floor conference room as my office.

It had a multi-million dollar view of the sparkling Pacific. "All mine!" I gloated, though the digs would of course be temporary because I was a temp. And I mention the "temp-ness" of my situation for a reason. Sometimes you can be paid exceptional money for a job for a short while. Companies can easily rationalize paying out significant sums, especially if you are consulting. If they feel you are working on a special project, or they are "leasing" your skills and services, they are inclined to justify the big bucks. Greedily, they're licking their chops because they see an end-date to your "over-market" ministrations.

Of course, your job is then much like Scheherazade's. Remember, she was the captured smarty-pants that was going to be put to death in the morning. But she told tales that were so riveting with such cliffhanging "endings," that she was allowed to live another day, to complete the dramas. Of course, one cliff led to another, and one evening to the next, and her life was constantly spared.

You can always generate enough projects for yourself if you are imaginative and you are capable. Think of it this way. Why would those that are hiring you shy away from future endeavors with you when you have had a positive track record with them? If they hired you, your glory is their glory, or at least this is how rational folks think.

But who said business folks are completely rational? There will always be downward pressures on your earnings. It is a truism in business that cost cutting is a perennial objective. "Can't we get someone else, someone cheaper to do what Gary is doing" is a constant refrain. Even if this isn't overtly asked, it is always a looming question.

And this means you need to prepare yourself to:

1. Sell the advantages of your initial project or job
2. Deliver those advantages
3. Publicize the results you have achieved
4. Sell new projects or add to your current slate of responsibilities.

"Better! Faster! Cheaper!" These are constant goals in businesses and organizations, with an emphasis on "Cheaper!" You need to be a moving target, harder to hit with the clipper of cost-cutters. If you remain at the same company, sooner or later you will be cut back in your wages, benefits, and then finally altogether axed.

Thus, change will be your constant companion. And before the accountants can nix your career in the bud, you need to do it for them. You need to make you, obsolete, before they do.

Before we leave this topic, let me underscore one of the activities I mentioned above: Publicizing the results you have achieved. I said you become visible if not conspicuous when you are one of the more highly paid people in an organization. But all visibility isn't bad.

It can help you when your contributions become widely known. People that learn about your pluses can become references to call upon later. You'll need references if you hope to rise in your current company and especially when you jump ship to another one.

If you cannot conspicuously "own" the results you have achieved, this will cost you money. I was doing a major consulting project that brought me to a company over the course of a few years. We were doing groundbreaking work, together. Masking the firm I was employed by, I wrote a case study of the success we were achieving in my subscription newsletter. I passed out free copies to employees at the company I was consulting for.

Why did I do this? I did it to create documented authorship of the results we were getting, earth shattering, cosmos changing results that would otherwise be owned exclusively by senior managers once my program came to its conclusion.

My pamphleteering didn't endear me to one of the division presidents who would certainly use our results to promote his career. But the internal publicity was worth the price I paid. And he went on to become the head of a huge bank and then a golden parachute retirement worth many millions.

If you want outstanding pay, realize this, you will stand out! This fact makes you a target, but if you have the right attitude about success, it will also become a magnet for bigger and better things. Not only did that division president land on his feet. I did, too, earning multiples of what I was paid at his firm. This windfall came to me largely based on the exceptional results I had achieved, and then publicized.

A client of mine at Xerox, who was very savvy and knew how to get things done at a big company put it nicely: "It is easier to ask for forgiveness than for permission!" To borrow from an economic philosopher, I might add, the question isn't "Who will let you," create your own high-paying job, but "Who will stop you?"

Tip 8:
A Word To The Wise Isn't Enough

A few years back one of my former clients called me out of the blue. An investor was in his office, and we were put on a speaker. My client said, "Gary I have a simple yes or no question I want to ask you." He explained that he had a new piece of consumer technology that he wanted to sell by phone. "Do you think it can be done?" he wondered.

Let me put his "simple yes or no question" into perspective.

I am the bestselling author of the book, *You Can Sell Anything By Telephone!* It is one of the field's most celebrated sources and it helped to launch the modern discipline of outbound selling. The title almost says it all. My inclination is to say anything can be sold by phone. So, my client probably thought it was a slam-dunk that I would respond this way.

My client also knew that I pulled no punches. If I felt a certain way about the results we were getting in the consulting program we did together, I was very forthright with my assessments. Thus my yes or no would be truthful and would have weight. He could rely on it to be sincere.

A silence ensued that was palpable. He was waiting for my answer, the proverbial word to the wise that would be sufficient. But there was a complication. Since I wrote that book I have done numerous phone campaigns promoting almost all kinds of products and services. One thing I came to realize is the challenge of telephone selling is made more difficult if you are promoting new, complex, or technological items to consumers, to non-experts.

You bear a burden of explaining clearly and persuasively something that could require a demonstration. The phone, as a medium, doesn't really have the ready capacity to create the clarity required to promote confidence and enable persuasion to take place.

To net this out, two tentative conclusions entered my mind as he described the product he was marketing: (1) He *could* sell the item, but (2) He might not sell enough units to be profitable.

I really needed more time to consider the matter and to determine what kind of script, if any, might be successful in meeting the challenge. So, I demurred. I said I wasn't comfortable giving him an answer at that moment and he needed to retain my services at my customary rate to fund the development of an informed reply. Minimally, a day or two would be needed for me to learn more about his product and to determine the scope of the challenge. He was impatient, couldn't wait, didn't want to pay, and the call was terminated.

From afar, I followed the telemarketing project that he went ahead and launched without my input. He and his investors, by my estimate lost millions of dollars. Comparatively, a small five-figure investment in research with me would have saved them a tremendous amount of time and effort that they could have redirected properly into the project, if I gave the green light, and away from that project, if I didn't.

There are lots of lessons in this tale. One of them echoes the old proverb about not being pennywise and pound-foolish. But from my standpoint as a professional, this story is emblematic of the difficulty of properly pricing one's work product if you are a "thinker" or if what your clients are buying is "judgment."

My almost instantaneous gut feeling, that (1) Yes, the item could be sold; but (2) You might not want to do it, came from years and years of experience. There was not only that response but also a track record I had developed with other companies "doing the impossible" over the phone.

For example, a major international electronics company was fielding thousands of complaints a day about its product. I was asked if there was a way to (1) Assuage the customers' anger; and (2) Sell the customers a new item during the same conversation.

This is a case study you should hear in its entirety but for now, let me say I found this one of the most interesting, theoretical and practical challenges of my career. I gave them a tentative yes, and outlined a program to develop a new technique for doing what they sought. They paid for development and then for a pilot program to test my method.

It succeeded beyond anyone's expectations. Fully 50% of the people we communicated with using the enhancements I developed purchased additional products. This campaign transformed a cost center into a profit center, which is pretty much equivalent to transforming base metal into gold; an alchemist's dream.

Informed by multiple successes of this magnitude, there wasn't a simple answer to my client's question. Any affirmative answer I gave would also have to contain this caveat:

Yes, you can sell this by phone but if you want to do it profitably, it should be done with my help.

I was practically born into telephone selling. My dad was great at it and I would listen to him making calls at home. Then, at 18, I became a full-time collector on the phone; at 19, a top sales rep with Time-Life, and still at 19 the youngest sales manager in their system.

I worked my way through three degrees, including a Ph.D. in Communication, enabling me to marry my real world experience with theory, to advance the state of the art. Therefore, when I hear a challenge, I know what I know, I know what I don't know, and I know what others do and do not know. But most importantly, I know how to systematically learn more and to innovate. I can solve problems that others cannot solve.

Thus, that client's question is tricky in this regard: *I* can address practically any challenge by telephone, but without my help, he could not. You know what you know, but no more. And you may be clueless about how to innovate.

But as long as you don't know what you don't know, you won't be able to know that a word to the wise may not even come close to being what you need to hear. People come to me all the time with an offer to buy an hour or two of my time. But time is not what they are after. If it were, they could roll up to the Home Depot and buy the time of a window washer for ten bucks an hour, or a handyman's time for twenty. They want judgment and expertise and frankly these things don't come cheaply.

A business relationship may be expressed in clock time, but that metric doesn't fairly capture the value clients are seeking or the value I am vending. Withholding my thinking from that former client cost him millions of dollars. He is upset with me to this day for not shooting from the hip or giving away my thinking, experience, and judgment for free.

Of course, I empathize. How could he know what was in my mind or what I was capable of achieving if he wasn't willing to pay to find out?

Tip 9:
Forget Past Boo-Boos

I was teaching my Best Practices in Negotiation seminar at UCLA last Saturday. For the hundredth time I thought about discussing an article that appeared in the *New York Times* back in 2012. What made this situation different was that I was teaching in a technology-enhanced room. With a few buttons I could search for the article and project it onto the large screen at the front of the class.

The article is titled, *"Praise is Fleeting, But Brickbats We Recall."* Brickbats are criticisms and other negatives. (March 23, 2012.)

The point is that bad news, reversals, negatives, job losses and miscellaneous career hurts are far more memorable to us than the successes we have achieved.

One of my seminar attendees, a banker by profession, mentioned he runs seminars for high-asset clients. These are folks with $250,000.00 or more under management with his bank. Because the bank charges fees that have a relationship to the amount of assets they manage, it is always a great objective to add more of these high-asset individuals to the flock. Thus, seminars are constructed that share some of the bank's current investment wisdom and recommendations. These programs are provided free to Private Banking clients, those with the bigger bucks. Inevitably, according to my attendee, along with the certified heavy hitters, some others slip in to his lectures for the free lunch and free advice. This irks him. He believes only Private Banking clients should be permitted to attend.

Of course, he faces a dilemma. If he casts these people out he could cause a scene and that would offend any heavy hitting friends that brought them along. Yet he wants to maintain the exclusivity of the group and get the freeloaders to pay their way by giving the bank more of their wealth to manage.

Yet, when all is said and done, he doesn't assess the success of his class based on how well the in-crowd reacted to it. He dwells on the pain he feels over the fact that he shared his wisdom "for nothing" with those that didn't belong.

In other words, the pain of loss is more motivating to him than the possibility of gain. This sounds crazy, but according to the article I mentioned and the research it cites, it is human nature. "Put another way," according to the article, "You are more upset over the loss of $50 than you are happy about gaining $50."

Across the water from where we live there are two benches. For the first time, my wife noticed a person laying down on one of them, covered by a blanket. That person was there for about five hours.

I made lunch for the family, including some soup and sandwiches for my children. One of my girls said, "I don't want egg salad sandwiches anymore. I want turkey." Well, it was too late. Egg salad was made and it was in front of them. And then, it hit me. Over the water there is a person that probably would be thrilled to eat the complainer's portion.

As a lesson in appreciation I mentioned this to my brat-child. (Later, her Mom would take a sandwich to that stranger, who expressed delight and appreciation.)

The entire episode brought back a very powerful memory. I was 18, on my own, and money was tight. I had a tiny apartment a block away from my favorite burger place, where I had been a busboy three years before.

I ordered a huge burger with pretty much my last nickels, dimes and quarters and a few singles. Suddenly, as it was being cooked, I fell ill. I had to get home, and in my hurry to leave enough to pay the check and the tip, I left most of that fine burger on the plate and scooted away. I really was sick!

I have never forgotten that uneaten meal, and the sacrifice I made in leaving it. The pain of sacrificing, of losing that wonder-burger has never left me! I can afford burgers galore as many adults can, but no matter how good they are they cannot blot out that memory of loss.

Another attendee at the same UCLA seminar mentioned how badly treated he was when he negotiated with a large, super well known company. That boo-boo, that hurt, has tainted practically every negotiation he has done since.

So, what does this have to do with you? You need to forget the bad jobs you have had in the past and especially those employers that told you your work was inferior or that your career would lead nowhere. This takes effort to do! I urged the banker and the other fellow to consciously remind themselves of all of their successes before negotiating their next paycheck or deal.

Research cited in the article says it takes at least *five* good happenings to take the sting out of one bad happening. Frankly, I think this figure is far too low. It might take ten or a hundred or even a thousand positives to counterbalance the injury done to our psyches by one bad event or perceived failure. Some people interviewed in the article keep a list handy that details their victories. After they experience a setback or a defeat, they pull out the list and slowly read it to themselves.

This tendency to over-emphasize the negative was also noticed by my mentor, famed management guru Peter F. Drucker. He said most of us waste time, energy, and money by trying to fix our weaknesses instead of accentuating our *strengths*. Schools are likely to steer students and parents to those grade in report cards that are less than stellar. "Alex really needs to work on this!" is the urgent advice. Practically no time addresses the fact that he or she has a gift in other areas.

Drucker says it is far easier to work to our strengths than to eliminate weaknesses. "Mozart shouldn't have spent a moment worrying about his math," Drucker quipped on more than one occasion. There are plenty of reason humans emphasize the negative, according to the article. But they should be muted by your voice that reminds you gently and repeatedly of your strengths.

Tip 10:
Should You Tell Anyone What You're Doing?

It is important to set high goals, what I call a challenging aspiration level for yourself.

When I was growing up I used to see an astonishing number of luxury cars: Rolls-Royces, Bentleys, Mercedes, Cadillacs, Ferraris, and other fine rides. Sometimes these cars were lined-up at a single streetlight. My dad drove a Chevy Convertible, still a very cool car to me, but it wasn't luxury class. I set a goal that one day I would purchase a Bentley Convertible. It would be dark red with that sumptuous ivory interior with piping matched to the exterior red color. To me, that was the epitome of class, style, and power.

I didn't get my first car until I won a leadership scholarship at community college. That prize enabled me to by my boss's very used VW Bug. Far from Bentley-class, right? But we have to start somewhere and believe me, that VW was a godsend. It got me to work and to classes on time and was the steed that transported my dates and me.

A few cars later, I was actually able to afford a top of the line, brand new Mercedes convertible. At the time it was the priciest model in their American lineup. Yes, it was in dark red with a great contrasting interior. Not a Bentley, but my tastes had changed, and I was more than okay with this rolling spectacle.

My point is you should also set a challenging aspiration level, a goal that is motivating enough to excite you. It should be dazzling enough that will get you out of bed in the morning, singing and clapping. It could be expressed in money. You could imagine that you're going to make $500,000 a year or more. I realize this could be far away from your current earnings, the sort of stretch from my VW to that Bentley or Mercedes convertible. Or, it could even be from taking a bus to those fine rides.

The fact that you have set it as an objective is what counts. When it becomes a goal, it is helpful to write it down, many pundits point this out. Once you have it, can see it before you, it becomes possible. Indeed, it becomes an imperative, which is a must-accomplish, must-do, must get item in your life. From that moment, you aren't lost at sea, buffeted about randomly by influences outside of your control. You have a vision of a distant shore. Then you can devise your map and resolve to stay on course. But most importantly, first comes the goal setting, the resolve to go somewhere important.

Now, let's say you have decided to earn that half-million. You have written it down. Do you share your goal with anyone else? Do you climb to a convenient rooftop and bellow your objective to anyone that will hear it?

There are two schools of thought on this topic. A "public declaration" is a powerful device because it signals commitment. It is like setting fire to the bridge that you have just crossed in your thinking, spanning what you will currently accept to what you are really going after.

In a sense, there is no going back, no retreating. Unless, that is you are willing to lose face, eat crow, and lose esteem not only in the eyes of others but also when you look in the mirror.

This isn't the worst of all worlds; I have to say. But it is certainly painful to the ego.

The other approach is to keep your own counsel, to "Lend thy ear but not thy tongue" to other people about your goal, as Shakespeare put it. Zipping your lip is really my temperamental preference. When I reveal my ambitions to most other people, I set up resistance. Wet blankets will quickly tell you your goal is not possible. They'll say, "Uncle Mikey tried something like that and he fell flat on his face. Never got over it!"

They might be trying to spare us the disappointment of failure, but in doing so they spare us its valuable lessons. Our skin doesn't get thicker by staying out of the elements, the typhoons of struggle. They could tell us we aren't fit for the adventure, and usually, they'll be projecting on us their own limitations. They are really saying that they aren't fit.

I decided to go to law school after I completed my Ph.D. and I was president of a successful consulting firm. Purposely, I didn't tell anyone in my family I was putting myself through this process. My mother didn't know. My sister didn't know.

Over four years after I had begun, I was already a licensed attorney by the time my graduating class walked through the ceremony in June. I had already graduated, early, and I sat successfully for the bar examination.

I sent out invitation to that event. "Why did you decide to go to law school?" they asked. Get this: They would have bugged me with that question, making me doubt my own resolve had I shared this intention four years earlier! I didn't want to put any obstacles between my goal and myself by announcing it.

I had a similar experience after my doctoral program. I launched my very successful consulting practice that provided among a number of other benefits that dark red Mercedes convertible I mentioned earlier. I invited my professor to lunch. Getting into that fine ride he asked, "Where did all of this come from?"

It came from a mind that set a goal and was smart enough not to ask others if my goal made sense to them. Go ahead and set a lofty goal, I say. The more ambitious it is, the better it will be. Again, write it down.

But do not share it with anyone that will fill your mind or heart with doubts. That's a long list, because envy is rampant. People will try to discourage you.

Why let them take the wind from your sails?

Tip 11:
Win That Job With The Law of Large Numbers

A few years ago, I recorded a very successful audio seminar (which is now also a book): *The Law of Large Numbers: How to Make Success Inevitable.*

The theme is very simple. The more you do, the more you'll get. Indeed, do enough of anything and you will succeed. Do more and you will prosper. Outdo even that effort and you'll become a legend.

I like to use as an example a fellow who worked with me at Time-Life. He was a successful salesperson, not a world-beater, but effective. His greatest gift was his intellectual curiosity. He always wanted to know how other local companies were doing their selling. He was especially interested in how their pay plans were set-up. Naturally, his question was, "Can I do the same thing that I'm doing at Time-Life and earn a lot more money?"

I commend you to ask this same question, given where you toil. I assure you, some company is paying premium wages right now to folks that have no more skills or experience than you have. Your ticket to creating a high-paying job could be simply seeking out these opportunities.

My colleague did this. But unlike most, he took his question to the extreme. He really wanted to know, "*where* can I earn more than what I'm being paid at Time-Life?" He scanned employment listings for all companies that seemed to be doing inside sales, our specialty at the time. He called them all, saying he was doing very well where he was but he wanted to know if they offered a better opportunity.

His effort was what I call a "Law of Large Numbers Campaign." Again, he wasn't putting the toe into the water. He plunged in, wading into office after office in search of a bigger and better deal. Here's what he found. There were people making a lot more money, as sales reps, than my people were making. In some cases, they were earning three and four times as much. He also found there was a price to be paid if he joined them. He would have to transition to being a straight commission seller. This means, when you sell, you are paid. When you don't, you starve! It's feast or famine, sometimes within the same day, week, or month. If you could handle the uncertainty that came with never knowing if you'd get a paycheck, you could do very well for yourself. Largely though, the risk-of-nonperformance was being shifted from the company to you.

This may seem unsettling to you. But if you have a lot of self-confidence, or you have been a successful seller almost everywhere you have worked, a straight-commission arrangement may be the cat's pajamas for you. In fact, one way to create a high-paying job would be to identify a company you want to work with that does *not* pay this way. Let's say they pay a small hourly wage plus bonuses, but you like them and sense they are going places.

You can turn the tables on them. Ask them to pay you a percentage of the revenue you bring in on a straight commission basis. For taking the risk of nonperformance onto yourself, you could earn far more than what the current people are being guaranteed.

Before you think this is extremely hazardous to your income or bank account, take a close look at what I just suggested. This is a company that is already succeeding to a point in selling its goods and services. So, you are relieved of the annoying concern, "Can this item be sold?" It is being sold. The company is simply not sharing enough of the proceeds with its staff. Part of the reason for being stingy is the company has to recruit, train, and terminate non-performers, paying them all the while. You are reducing their financial risks by willingly taking on the straight commission formula. Moreover, you are implicitly saying you will out-sell their current staff. And you probably will. Here's why.

You will have a greater financial incentive and you'll know you must sell to eat. You'll always be on your toes, trying your best.

Let's get back to my associate. He received tons of job offers. This is due to his great application of The Law of Large Numbers. Implicitly, he knew the more companies he approached, the more interviews he would have. And from those multiple interviews multiple offers would come his way.

I think he didn't bolt from his current Time-Life deal for several reasons. One of the most significant was prestige. Time-Life was a great company, part of Time, Incorporated, and a vast publishing empire that would morph into Time Warner. Also, I think he was a bit of a security freak. The idea of a straight commission deal scared him. He didn't trust a lot of the companies with which he interviewed to actually pay him all of his earnings.

Flash forward about a year, and he made the leap. He went to the straight commission side of the sales force and he earned well. He beat what we were paying him, and his hours were more flexible.

A footnote to this story is why he succeeded as well as he did in generating new opportunities for himself. Frankly, he was a little bit on the introverted side. In a former era, he might have been called bookish. (We were working for the book division of Time-Life, so that is a fitting descriptor, indeed!) He succeeded because he *didn't care* if he found a better job. He wasn't ego-invested in the outcomes of those contacts he made, or the interviews that followed. This take-it-or-leave-it-but-mostly-leave-it attitude paid off. One of the most attractive qualities you can project is the self-confidence coming with what sociologists call role-distance.

When you are a job seeker you're in a role much like an actor on stage. There are certain attitudes that are typical of most job seekers. Humility and neediness are two of them. If you are completely in your role, you will project these to potential employers and they will surmise that they can underpay you. So, instead of creating a high-paying job you will perpetuate low-paying job offers.

When you have role-distance, you send two signals. Surely, you are there to discuss opportunities and if there is a good job offered you'll take it. At the same time you are projecting a meta-attitude, an above-attitude. This one says: "I don't have to say yes, I have other choices, and I'll take them unless you pay me a lot more than you're used to paying."

Don't get me wrong. You aren't coming across as superior to the people you're speaking to. You are superior to inferior offers, though!

When you have only one interview scheduled at one company and there are no more on the horizon, then it is almost impossible to have role-distance. "I really, really need this!" is what you're telling yourself, and this is also being communicated, at least nonverbally, to the interviewer.

This is why it is critical to do a Law of Large Numbers job seeking campaign. Your role-distance and power will be directly correlated with the number of other options you have. If you are legitimately convinced there are lots of other fish in the sea, then you'll give yourself a huge advantage.

Tip 12:
Make It A Game!

I mentioned the guy that worked for me at Time-Life. I highlighted the fact that he used the Law of Large Numbers in his pursuit of higher paying opportunities. Making more and more and more money is fun, so he transformed it into a game. This is exactly what billionaires do, and so should you. After all, think about those rich folks. A billion equals one thousand millions. Even one million is pretty good dough. Ten is far better. One hundred million and how could you ever run out of cash even if you bought the toniest Gucci and Versace bags? But a billion? Who the heck needs a billion? They do, because they don't strictly speaking need it. They want it, and they want it because it is a game for them.

It is a prize, a goal, a sought-after outcome, and maybe it is the answer to a long-held dream. What does it matter? It is fun to him, and it was fun to Buddy, the guy that worked for me at Time-Life. He got a big kick out of getting better and better, more and more highly paid job offers. And they came to him in profusion.

I said that happened in part because he had role-distance. He didn't care one way or another if he succeeded at getting a new job. He didn't need one or really want one: He wanted to be wanted. Being sought after, being alluring to employers was a heady kick to him. Some folks crave celebrity. Buddy wanted to be coveted by potential employers that thought he would be the ticket to spiked profits. If they brought him in he would produce. But more importantly, he would kick the complacent butts of those that were kicking back, living off the fat of the land, vegging on the company's largesse. He'd be a symbol of management's competence, a sure signal that said, "See, we can replace any of you at any time.

Whether they'll admit it or not, what most bureaucrats crave is the ability to look at their best producers and say, ho-hum, give me a hassle and you're done. Their relationship to top performers is always one of love and hate, simultaneously. They love the production, but they hate being beholden to anyone, and especially to temps. Managers and owners alike think of their employees as slaves of convenience, souls that can be wrung for all they're worth and then be discarded.

So, someone like Buddy, or *you* for that matter, comes along and says. "Hey I'm a great role model. I improve everyone around me. I'm just what you need. I'll immediately set the bar higher. Hire me not only because I'm great by myself and I'll be a big-time contributor, but because our people will have a new leader that sets a faster pace.

So, your role in this otherwise Machiavellian nightmare is to turn the tables. This isn't their game to enjoy; it is yours to relish.

When I started my consulting practice, or more aptly, when it started me, I had no clue as to what I could charge for my fee. The first gig I had was an offshoot of my teaching at Cal State Northridge, where I earned the princely sum of $25 an hour for helping a medical association to develop its speaker's bureau.

I had a good time at that but it provided little guidance as to what I could charge. My next gig happened when I was teaching in Indiana. I was invited for a day to consult at a Los Angeles home health care company. I may have charged them $1,000 for the day, which was close to what I took home by the month at my professor gig, so I was in splendor.

But these experiences did nothing to guide me in setting my wages a year or two later when I morphed full-time into a consultant. In fact, when people that would attend my seminar asked me, "What would you charge to do this seminar at my company?" I froze-up. I knew it was a compliment, but I hadn't given any deep thought to what my pay scale should be.

At some point I happened upon $1,750 a day. That seemed like a good figure, and it really was. I sold hundreds of days at that rate and most buyers were happy with it. Only one gent in LA said, "Why the average consultant only charges $1,500 a day," to which I replied, as I have shared already, "Well, I'm not average!" Apart from him, $1,750 was easy-peasy-lemon-squeasy. Which means, it was probably below or far below market.

If there is very little or no pushing-back on the fees or wages you ask for, believe me, you are giving away your labor and expertise too cheaply. You need to test a higher price, and this is where the fun comes in. What we don't know until we try is the answer to this question, what is too high?

I went to $2,250 a day and I sensed some resistance. It took a little longer to get deals approved. A slight amount of resistance occurred. But I got it, fairly consistently. Let's look at that price increase. I bumped the $1,750 up by $500. $500 into $2,250 is 22.22%. That's a modest way to test the market, going up by a mere 20% or so. Try that.

If you're in a wage situation earning $30 an hour, go to $36. It's not much of a bump to them, if they're serious about you. But it can have a huge impact on your earnings and lifestyle.

And of course the question is this: Did I lose 20% of my revenue by going up 20%? More often than not, the answer will be no. From there, keep edging up. Sooner or later, you'll experience a big drop-off of demand.

This does not mean you should take the resistance or flack, personally. You shouldn't. Remember, raising prices is a game you should enjoy playing. When it stops being fun, there are better ways to create a high paying opportunity. And what you charge, doesn't always make what you earn, go up. We'll turn to that later on.

Tip 13:
Create Your Dream Job

There is a saying that there is no greater influence on a person than the unfulfilled dreams of his or her parents. My dad wanted me to become a professional baseball player. He had played minor league ball and he tried out with the Detroit Tigers. They had an impressive American League team.

Like several things in life, many are called but few are chosen. Dad didn't make it. For quite some time, he showed a lot of restraint in directing me to that unfulfilled aspiration. I don't even recall playing catch with him. Most of my athletic learning experiences came on playgrounds and playing fields. But I was a natural athlete, taking to every sport very easily. Baseball, by far was my favorite. I could have played it all year long, but in those days we didn't have the specializations that we have today. So, I played the cycle: football, basketball, and baseball as the seasons would come and go.

Somewhere around ten something went off in my brain telling me I simply had to get a lot better at baseball. Like many kids I dreamed about hitting game-winning homeruns and saving the day by making spectacular catches in the field. I started practicing with Irv, who was a year older and a phenomenal athlete. He would go on to play in the White Sox organization. He was fast, wiry, and surprisingly strong for his age. And he turned out to be a great mentor. I developed well and quickly under his guidance.

The proof of the pudding would come when Little League tryouts came up. I couldn't wait. On the appointed day throngs of youngsters in my age group assembled at Roxbury Park, on the field where games were held. Standing on the edge of the outfield grass, coaches hit fly balls to us, one at a time. Then they would quickly mark their scorecards.

My turn came and the ball was hit way, way over my head. Instantly, the coach that smacked it said, "Forget it!" thinking that he'd hit me another, one that was catchable. But I quickly turned toward the fence and ran at full speed with head down toward the spot where the ball was heading. Then I left my feet and stretched out my body and snared the ball in my glove at the very last split second.

The crowd cheered, even the kids that were acutely competitive, the ones that thought my gain was their loss. It was simply a magnificent baseball moment, something you'd go to a major league park to see but maybe only once every fifty or hundred games the pros would put on a display like I did.

From that point, destiny seemed to be in my corner. After that catch, my pal, Bobby said, "Not bad, Goodman!" I knew he wanted to be a pitcher, and in my cockiest tone I made a bold prediction. "The first time I face you as a hitter I'm going to put one over the center field fence." "No way," he smiled back.

The day finally arrived. He played for the Cardinals and I was on the Dodgers. He was brought in as a relief pitcher and I was in the on deck circle. When I stepped into the batter's box, I smiled and tilted my head toward center field. He suppressed a grin of his own. With a two-and-one count I reached for a fastball on the outside corner. It sailed high above the field toward, you guessed it, dead center field. Seemingly floating forever it plunked down outside of the fence for a home run. Just as I so arrogantly predicted, I hit a homer, in my first at bat against Bobby. And more unbelievably, I poked it to dead center field.

What were the odds? And how could I have predicted it a year or more, before?

My dad somewhat suddenly took interest in my Little League games. I should mention he was concerned I'd get hurt and he resisted my even trying out. But now, I seemed destined for greatness. He told me later that the New York Mets scouted me as a 12-year old. Their dictate to him was clear: Just keep Gary in baseball. As you might tell, I found dad's sudden interest in my exploits self-serving. They added to his glory and he became a popular socialite in the stands during games. This is from a fellow that was otherwise reserved and detached. Now, he was an extrovert and happy to shake the outstretched hand after I did something good.

During his most glorious year as my sports-dad, when I was 12, I set some records across the country according to the president of Little League. I captained the All-Star team, and my batting average was an impressive .582. I also led the league in walks, and I came in second in total home runs, missing a tie by one stroke. I even got a chance to pitch a game. I had been bugging our coach and he finally gave in.

I wasn't the type to pitch a no-hitter. I was a catcher, usually. And I was almost late for my pitching start. Hitchhiking to the park, a nice young chap in a Corvette broke the land speed record in getting me there all of seven minutes before game time.

Quickly, I warmed up and then the game was on. Our opponents scored four runs, which on most days would have been a winner for them.

My team scored nine runs, and here's how we did it. I hit three homeruns, and knocked in eight of our nine runs by myself. I almost hit four homers. In my third at bat I picked up the wrong piece of wood. I hit that ball to the fence, but he reached up and pulled it down.

Thinking something was wrong I started blaming the bat, at least in my mind. I looked at it more closely and saw it was one inch smaller than my usual stick. My final at bat that day I made sure to pick up the right bat, and sure enough, that's when I collected my third homer of the day.

I had hit a homerun during the last at bat of the previous game, as well. So when you add up all of those pluses, four homers out of five at bats, pitching the complete game, and so on, that's where one of my records came from, said the league president.

I regale you with this story of my baseball glory for a purpose. I would not go on to play pro ball as my dad had come to ardently wish. Indeed, between Pony League and my senior year of high school I dropped out of sports. I felt I was achieving in that realm for my dad and not for myself. I had enjoyed the game, but I didn't want to be pushed. It wasn't fun anymore. It was becoming serious, like a profession.

At 17, at my dad's prodding, after high school I played briefly in the lowest rungs of the Los Angeles Angels organization. I was not in peak playing condition. Significantly older and stronger players outgunned me. I wouldn't achieve full maturity in strength, weight or height until four or five years later. Quickly, it was clear to me that my time in the sport had come and gone.

When the topic comes up, which it only rarely does these days and people ask why I didn't go farther in the game, I simply say, "I wasn't good enough." That is, strictly speaking, true. But the better explanation is that my heart wasn't in it. Professional baseball stopped being my dream. When it started to become professional, like a job-job, the fun was gone.

When you are creating a high-paying job, make sure that you are enthusiastic about what it is that you're choosing to do.

Above all, check to make sure it is your dream job, and not someone else's dream for you.

Tip 14:
It's Okay To Reject Bad Offers

I've been corresponding with a prospect about doing some work for his company as a consultant. He has told me that my quoted hourly rate is well beyond what he pays his distinguished attorney. I don't want him as a law client. I want him as a sales or customer service client. You'll need to trust me when I tell you there is a big difference.

Some folks that could be great sales or customer service clients would make irritating and nit-picking law clients. Finally, he rejected a three-hour offer I made to him that would have enabled us to start a formal relationship. He came back saying he'd buy one hour, but only at a discount. Normally, I don't charge by the hour, at all, as I responded in a cover note. I'm not going to share with you my full reply to him, the purpose of which was to get him away from "hourly" thinking and onto "value" thinking.

Changing people's perceptions of your value and what they need to pay for is challenging. But it is necessary if you want to create a high-paying job or opportunity for yourself. My note concluded by saying someone like my prospect came to me years ago, and instead of purchasing a day or two of my time, he decided to go it alone. He lost millions of dollars, being pennywise and pound-foolish.

What was the point of sending this extensive piece, which I wrote on a customized basis for him to read? It took me more than an hour of time to compose, an hour that I could have billed him for had I invested it in a phone call. I forwent his offer of buying an hour of my time, not only to send the message that hourly is not how I work. I was able to refer both generally and specifically, to my great success in taking on customized consulting projects.

It took him about a week to respond. I was used to that. I sense he shared the contents of my emails with family members, who are also in his business. He said, essentially, (1) He has a problem in marketing; (2) It is important and he hasn't been able to solve it; and (3) He's open to getting my help.

These are three admissions that people who can pay you an exceptional income need to make. Once they hear or see themselves making these admissions, they have taken a crucial step. They are acknowledging their need and including us in the ownership of their challenge. Implicitly, they are also saying they'll share some of the treasure a solution will provide if we can help them out.

They are thinking about value that they'll get by relieving their problem, and as long as the cost of doing so is less than the value of that relief, they will probably move forward with us. To put this into a dollar perspective, let's say you are solving a $100,000 problem for someone. How much will they pay for this benefit? We can say they'll pay a proportion of $100k. Easily, $20–30K comes to mind. Others will pay half or more, $50K and up.

As you get closer to the $100K mark, they're thinking about the other costs involved in implementing your solution, so they're probably backing off. We can say pretty much unequivocally, no one will pay $101K to solve a $100K problem, right? There is a limit to the value you can confer and that limit is governed by the value they are getting. Let's say you can save or earn for a company the sum of $1 million. Easily, you can demand $200,000.00 or $300,000.00 for that benefit.

Your job is to find or develop high-value situations that you can improve. The greater the need, the more costly it is to live with, the more you can charge as a fee or a salary to address it.

This means you are not going to get a dry cleaner to pay you a six-figure income if the owner doesn't earn that much. Be prepared to receive inferior offers for your time and labor and abilities. However, look to these occasions as reality tests. They could be signifying that the places you are looking for high-paying opportunities simply don't have them. There isn't any additional income to share.

Or, opportunities for big paydays are there, but you haven't defined them in a way those that pay will readily or gladly acknowledge. That's when you write a note such as the one I just described to you.

Tip 15:
Bad Jobs Push Out Good Jobs

When you have very little of anything, and it gives you at least some benefits, you struggle to hold on to it. You make it stretch, like the last doughnut in the box, or the final leftover meatball.

Jobs are like this, too. The worse they are for you, the more preciously we treat them. Let's say you're just teetering on the edge, barely paying your bills. The job that's supporting your brinkmanship seems absolutely essential. And it is, if you want to persist in just existing from day to day. But what it is also doing is pushing out good jobs. This becomes more apparent at higher rungs of the occupational food chain.

I tell this story to my negotiation students. I delivered a rollicking speech to a convention of franchisees from an international placement company. I earned my sizeable speaking fee, and a franchisee invited me to consult for its Connecticut location. One of my consulting formats is to do a two-day needs-assessment. On day one, I interview managers. I also assess the capabilities of the other personnel. On day-two I report to the owners my perceptions and recommendations. If I believe my skills can be put to good use to solve any problems I detected, I'll suggest a specific course of training and development to address them.

In almost every situation I can remember, there has been something to fix, and I've gone ahead and offered to fix it, at an additional fee. This is customary, a part of the natural order of consulting, as I see it.

But on this occasion, something went wrong. The owner lied to me. He was married to one of the senior managers and this didn't come out until the end of the visit. This fact shook me up, because I am not used to this sort of fabrication.

I am a believer in "The Iceberg Theory." This says if what you see on the surface is treacherous, what you don't see, below the surface, is potentially devastating. I decided I would end the engagement at the two-day point and not return. Recall if you will, I was under no obligation to continue, though for me, it was customary.

The couple that owned the franchise was quite upset. They couldn't see why I chose to desist, and I really didn't want to disclose the fact that "It is because you are liars, and I don't care to work with liars." That would have made things worse, so I simply said I'm going to turn my attention to other clients.

Strictly speaking, that excuse bordered on being a fib. I didn't have another client clamoring for my time. I turned down what would have been serious money from that couple without having a Plan B.

Returning to California, I attended my customary class with management guru Peter F. Drucker at the school named in his honor at Claremont Graduate University. There, one of my classmates, Bob, worked for a major financial company. I mentioned the Connecticut episode to him and he said, "Why don't you do something for us?" His division was local, and I ended up doing a consulting gig for them that exceeded the dollar value of the Connecticut offer. And it began at the same time as I would have done the faraway program, but I didn't have to travel. So, I landed on my feet. The moral to the story is that there wouldn't have been the financial company engagement had I gone ahead with Connecticut. I had to relinquish the bad to create an opening for the good.

My level of risk in doing this doesn't seem as great as it is for that person I mentioned earlier that is in a bad job and is barely paying the rent. I knew, sooner or later, I'd consult again, and I'd find better clients for whom to do it. But in reality, the same facts apply to us all. We have to take our feet off of first base to steal second, putting it in baseball terminology. And that means there will be a gap of vulnerability that will be created. We might trip and fall on our faces as we tear for second. We could get thrown out by the catcher, or picked off by the pitcher, or stuck in a pickle somewhere between first and second while being chased by two or three opponents. Lots of things can go wrong!

But if we want to score, to improve our circumstances, we have to give up the lesser to get to the greater. The reason I use the Connecticut story in my negotiation classes is that it stands for many things. One of them is the importance of setting high aspiration levels. Another is the need to deal with honest people and companies.

But the third point addresses the question, "When is a negotiation done, finished, over with?"

I thought that episode with the franchisee was dead and gone. But the franchisor, the parent company, that had brought me in to speak at the initial convention contacted me. They asked me if I was willing to do a series of 12 speeches at their California headquarters for franchisees they would fly in.

We came to an agreement and I did the first one, a success. Then, I received a call from headquarters. They said they did not want to proceed with the remaining programs. After expressing surprise and pointing to the excellent ratings the first group gave me, my contact revealed this. The Connecticut franchisee refused to attend and was putting up a stink about the fact that HQ retained me to do the speaking series. They were buckling to pressure and wanted to be relieved of their obligation to continue.

I had reserved the dates and I turned down other engagements, so I didn't cave in. I demanded they "Play me or pay me." I knew I was within my rights. Between their gigs, I attended law school and passed the bar exam. So, this company was trying to get away with breaching a contract with an attorney. I let them know this, explicitly, and they were buying a lawsuit if they did not pay.

They paid, and a handsome payment it was. How much was it? Let me put it this way. I went to a fine private law school over the course of three and a half years. The tuition was pricey. The check they sent me covered all of the tuition that I had paid for law school.

So, out of good came bad, but out of that bad, came good, and then more bad, and then more good! Remember this: Don't be afraid, ever, to improve your job circumstances. The reason we feel we have to cling to the lesser is that we believe there is no greater. But there is, always. And by the way, a negotiation never ends!

Tip 16:
Should You Ever Work For Free?

I am probably one of the best salespeople you could ever meet. I've sold an extraordinary expanse of items. I've sold business-to-consumer and business-to-business. I've sold tangible products like ballpoint pens and news-papers, and intangible services. I've sold real estate. I've sold cars. I've also set appointments for other people to sell things like security bars for windows and doors.

And what I haven't sold directly, I've sold indirectly, having worked with the insurance business and wide swaths of the financial industry as a consultant. Well, you get the picture. If I haven't sold it all, I've sold "most" of it.

But there was one thing that I didn't sell well. It was gold and silver. I invested about six weeks on the phone hawking precious metals and I did not earn a dime. I was on a straight-commission compensation plan, and as I've said elsewhere, when you are paid this way, if you sell, you eat. If not, even that McDonald's unit that was next door to the metals place seemed like it had a pricey menu.

There are a lot of excuses I can cite to explain my lack of success. The leads were more than a year old, and they had been called and re-called, over and over. The market for gold and silver was in the tank. The stock market, which is a rival investment venue, was rising. Indeed, it was in a bull market phase. Inflows of free cash were going there. Gold and silver prices were tanking, moving down to their lowest levels in years. And really, no one around me was making any money, either, except an old-timer in the back of the room who relied on reloading his preexisting clients.

Here is the learning point: Sometimes you simply don't fit a given opportunity. It is possible that another seller in my shoes could have thrived at that place at that time. I doubt it, but it is possible. Nobody worked harder or made more calls than I did.

But the real point I want to make here is that the faster you realize a job is not going to work for you, the better off you will be. Once that thought hits you, pay attention! A lot of people, especially folks like me that have been trained as athletes, believe in the maxim memorialized in the parody, "Galaxy Quest," that says: "Never give up; never surrender!" When the going gets tough, the tough get going.

You know these slogans, and they hold true providing there has been some success before with that opportunity. However, there is the very real possibility that if you haven't cracked the nut within a reasonable period, as my dad used to say, you never will. In retrospect, I feel having invested 6 weeks at the metals place was about three weeks too many. Remember, I didn't see anyone else making money. That is a very bad sign. Prospects weren't calling me back in sufficient numbers, so I wasn't having enough meaningful conversations. And when I did reach folks, they seemed indifferent-to-hostile. They were not suitable metals buyers.

We waste too much time blaming ourselves in these situations.

"I *should* be succeeding!" we tell ourselves. In the meantime, we are taking on more water instead of paddling to shore. One interesting thought about that metals experience is that it is quite possible that I would be "a natural" at selling gold and silver, but only at another company. They did not invest in quality leads and given the fact that telephone calls are so cheap as to be practically free to make, and they were paying only based on performance, management had little incentive to improve matters. They were in the investment business but they failed to invest in their own sales process. But this wasn't necessarily the case across the street, at a different precious metals dealer. They might have had fresh leads. They might have paid a guaranteed wage against commissions, or a wage plus commissions. In other words they may have had a better deal going, one where sellers were actually selling! One bad experience shouldn't deter you from trying something similar, again, providing the key variables that contribute to success are in place.

You might have a bad manager in the tool business, but this isn't a commentary about every manager in the tool business. It could be a great place to earn an exceptional living, but our tendency is to generalize. There is significant research that says our tendency to be "Once burned and twice shy," is universal. And it could even be hardwired into us.

There is survival value in avoiding situations that are traps, injurious, or punishing in any way. So, according to theorists, we tend to be more attuned to negative feedback than to positive. Once something bad happens, we are super-diligent in trying to assure that it won't happen again. Another way of putting this is we are far more disappointed about losing a hundred dollars than we are about earning a hundred dollars. That bad experience selling metals had the potential of not only leading me to believe I could never sell gold and silver, anywhere. It made me risk generalizing that I am not the first-class, super-successful seller I had believed point that I was.

If you think I'm going to finish this tale by saying I did cross the street and I did jump back into selling precious metals, I'm going to disappoint you. I didn't, I haven't and I probably won't. There are too many better opportunities for me to pursue. And the market for metals overall seems to be shrinking, not growing. I have come to believe that it is a pretty dumb investment, so my heart wouldn't be in it.

Overall I believe it is possible that I could succeed in that field despite the fact that I failed. We should not take one data point, one experience and generalize from it. Don't let one failure define you. Like me, you could be the greatest seller in the world. You just won't prove it at that particular company. Find others, inside or outside of that field.

Tip 17:
Will You Get A Shot At Something Big?

Actor John Hamm, famous for his eight year role in the TV hit, *"Mad Men,"* is a poster-person for being a 12-year overnight success. That's how long it took this dashing former athlete to make it big. Of course, in retrospect, all of that incubating before hatching success seems oddly unnecessary. The guy looks destined to be a movie star. He *was* ad-man Don Draper, the guy he played on that hit TV show. This isn't to say Hamm scored zero roles until his breakthrough. He had one line in a movie, in the year 2000. He was in theater productions. He even did some work in designing movie sets. In other words, he got by until getting his big break.

Almost everybody that makes it big found a way to make it small, at first, to pay the bills and keep their heads above water. What we can say about actor Hamm is that he had upside potential as a being well-educated, well spoken, and handsome. He was playing in an arena where fame and fortune could find him. This is critical.

Let's say you have to take a job for minimum wage. Pay almost doesn't get any lower than that. You can make that minimum at a small micro-business that cannot afford to pay you any more than that. So, your big bang would be to get a one or two dollar raise. What is that going to buy you? Or, you could work for a movie theater chain, pulling down those small bucks. At least you'd get a chance to see every new feature, free.

And if you were an actor, you'd have a connection to show business, albeit a remote one. You could eat limitless popcorn and drink more cola than you'd ever want. In other words, there would be at least a small upside to where you were laboring. If you worked in a library or a bookstore, nobody would criticize you for reading when you had some free time. That would be a perk. Not much, but it is something.

Let's say you have absolutely no experience in selling, in fact, you hate the idea of doing it. And you could become the worst seller that ever asked someone to buy. If you were being paid minimum wage, of course you would get that. But it would be likely if you were working for a rational company that you could also qualify for commissions and bonuses.

Let me be clear. This fact wouldn't transform you into John Hamm, who went from obscurity to fame and co-invented binge watching of TV shows along with Netflix. But it would deliver an upside. While you were failing at that sales job, you would be learning your craft in the same way Hamm learned his, doing theatrical roles and scene design.

You would be paying some dues, and if you stayed at it long enough you would become competent. That means you would earn commissions and bonuses, transforming what was a minimum wage gig into a better opportunity. And of course, you could rise in the ranks to sales management and general management, once you succeeded in sales. Big oaks can grow from tiny acorns, because it is in their DNA to do so. You need to look for and create opportunities that will guarantee you the get-by, an okay return on your time, talent and energy. But you need to be playing that hand to win, to achieve much more than the bare bones get-by.

I don't normally advise people that are looking to create a high-paying job to work for start-ups, companies that don't have a prior track record of success. I am especially wary about those that try to staff with student or intern labor. As I have said elsewhere, they may throw "dog treats" at you, free snacks and coffee, and such. But what is likely to occur is they will exhaust their capital and fail. Or, if they succeed and are bought out by bigger entities, you won't see a dime extra when the few founders and insiders rake in the spoils. In the meantime, you'll be worked to death. They'll advertise a "work-hard and play-hard culture" that will be tilted dramatically toward the work-hard polarity.

There are some exceptions. If they have an existing and achievable stock option program, where you are given a chance to accumulate *equity*, or the right to buy that equity at a future date at a deep discount, then you could find yourself smack in the middle of John Hammland; the corporate equivalent. You could go from rags to riches. Your minimum wage work could suddenly be re-monetized when that start-up goes public.

I worked with a fellow who was one of the first hires at Sun Microsystems. For one reason or another, he quit and joined another tech company, which he also quit.

Had he stayed at Sun, he would have become incredibly wealthy because the initial hires were rewarded handsomely for their early contributions, before Sun's success was assured.

This scenario has played out again and again at companies such as Apple, where employees that bought stock became uber-rich. Ask yourself, "Do I have a shot at something *big* if I come to work for this firm?" You have to be careful. There are lots of companies that become household names but their glory days are well behind them. Now, they are on the down slope of success. I consulted for this kind of company more than once.

Going to work for one East Coast firm was a real score. Employees were hired permanently after an initial screening period. Then, according to the firm's handbook, even inept or slacking folks could never be fired. This was a public company, and employees could make a lot from their stock options, at least this was possible when the firm boomed. But twenty years after its initial launching, it was on the skids. Joining then would have been a huge career mistake. Would you have had a shot at something *big*, at that point? Not a chance and worse, if you put that tanking tech firm on your resume, it would have been a bad place to have come from.

Sometimes, a company in decline will indirectly offer excellent guidance about where you should hitch your wagon. When I consulted for another major tech firm its employees were angry because Apple seemed to have adopted their graphical user interface, commonly known as desktop icons, for personal computing. Where was the better place to be: at the firm with the complainers that felt ripped-off or at Apple? Another consulting client was miffed with Microsoft. They felt the Microsoft product was inferior to theirs. That client sold out to another software firm. But Microsoft went on to achieve industry dominance.

One guideline to affiliating with a firm that can offer you something *big* is to do a jealousy-check. What companies are other companies complaining about? Don't join the chorus of complainers. Instead, join those that are the objects of their jealousy. You will improve your odds of creating a much higher-paying job!

Tip 18:
Will The Money Follow
If You Do What You Love?

Philosopher Joseph Campbell suggests to happiness seekers: "Leap, and a net will appear!" In other words, follow your bliss and great things will come to you. Is there any truth in this idea? Should you go boldly in the direction of your dreams as another philosopher urges, and will thousands of helping hands support you along the way? I can find some support for this theory in my career, but we'll get back to that in a minute.

First, let's talk about Tom, who was a middle manager with an airline when our paths crossed. He hired me to do a sales training program for most of the carrier's domestic locations. It was a good program, and it would pave the way to more lucrative contracts. But one of the long-lasting takeaways wasn't my success, but rather it was Tom's.

It was pretty clear to him that he wasn't going to climb into senior management where he worked. So, he picked up a number of side gigs. He sold me a cord of firewood, for example. Don't ask how he got into that sideline, but the wood lasted forever, and it burned about as well as expected, so I had no complaint. He also invested in a mini-market at a gas station. That move completely puzzled me. I couldn't envision Tom standing behind the counter, asking people, one after another, "Anything else with your Cheetos?" But he had a super-rational, simple explanation: "It's a good business, and I can sell it later, at a profit. In the meantime, it provides income." He went on to say he hired a manager who in turn hired an assistant manager and thus, Tom hardly ever had to do any heavy greeting.

I came to realize Tom and I were very different. I was following my bliss, which included traveling here and there, giving speeches and seminars, being called "Dr. Gary," and taking off from work over long stretches of time as I saw fit. Tom was 99% about making money, and becoming commercially successful. After all, he went to business school and he taught marketing at a local university, also part-time. There didn't seem to me to be anything he *wouldn't* do to earn a buck. I could imagine him investing in a laundromat while owning a piece of the car wash across the road. Cash flow, building equity, diversifying his portfolio, never getting bogged down in a single enterprise, all of these strategies and more were his strong suit.

Of course, I thought he was selling out for the almighty buck. There had to be a zillion things I wouldn't do, or that I once did in my teens but never again. ("Want fries with that?") Tom was totally agnostic when it came to his money worshipping. It didn't matter from whence the dollar streams flowed, as long as they flowed to him. It didn't occur to me until years later that *this was Tom's bliss.* He wasn't pretending to like all of his activities, but he may have been in clover. Having his fingers in a million pies could have been and probably was nirvana for Tom.

Speaking of bliss, someone once said, "Having money in the bank gives me a tremendous Zen feeling." Forget sackcloth and ashes, self-flagellation and self-denial. Beaucoup bucks could suit some people very well. Should you follow your bliss? Sure, and it could simply doing the oddest collection of things imaginable from other people's points of view. They don't matter.

What I can say is if your *only* rationale for working at a certain job or task is getting the paycheck, and you otherwise hate every minute of your endeavors, that will not be sustainable. I have been on certain consulting projects that were almost pure misery. I did not respect the people and the feeling was mutual. Every morning took a huge act of will to get me out of my hotel room, into the rental car, and off to these sites. We can do something sub-optimal for a while, or during wartime, or to save our families or ourselves from great distress. And that old saying, "Hard work never killed anybody" seems to apply here. Still, the hardest work in the world is work that you hate. And it isn't simply that the jobs are not glamorous.

This gets me back to Tom. The airline was glamorous. He, along with other executives, dressed nicely, as did I. There were no noxious fumes to be sniffed as there were at Tom's mini-market. But for me, I couldn't blend the odd cocktail that Tom drank every day. Being an airline exec, a firewood salesman, a mini-market maven, and everything else, all of these activities were too incongru-ous to me.

The theme of my live was, and still is to a large extent, generating and sharing new ideas for people and companies to be productive. It is mind work. The most physical it gets is presenting a dynamic lecture where I break a sweat, or pounding a keyboard as I write my current book or audio project. What I do must fit the theme of my life. If I am suddenly scooping ice cream at a mini-market instead of researching a topic online or at a library, I am oddly out of place. I'm wearing the wrong uniform. People don't regard me the same way. I feel dif-ferently about myself. My bliss is amiss!

Dr. Srully Blotnick wrote a book that I recommend to you, one that speaks to this bliss indirectly: *Getting Rich Your Own Way*. He tracked the careers of about 200 people over a 20-year period. He analyzed who got rich and who didn't. You would think that people that went into a "hot field" such as finance or technology came out far ahead of everyone else. Not so, according to Blotnick.

The people that grew rich found something the liked and they stayed with it, for the long term. Typi-cally, they got so good at it that they were able to attract more money for their labors. And they invested this extra money in typical places, including stocks and bonds and real estate. Most of them were unaware of how rich they were! Wealth snuck up on them while they were busy doing what they really liked to do.

I suppose an alternative title Blotnick could have used would be, *Follow Your Bliss & Grow Rich*, which is what pretty much happened to the cohort of folks he studied. Tom's example tells me there are exceptions to the rule. He became jack-of-all-trades and did quite well. And making money any old way seemed to be his bliss. Whether it is a means to wealth or the end being pursued, really enjoying what you do is a very helpful and often necessary condition of succeeding.

Tip 19:
Replace Scarcity Thinking
With Abundance Thinking!

When you look at the amount of money in your checking account, do you flinch or groan or avert your eyes? That's typical. And there are very few people that wouldn't be happier if they saw a few more zeroes. I don't have enough money!" you may tell yourself. This could be true if you're behind in your bills or rent. But from this statement, some people conclude that there is a shortage of money around us, in the community, nation, or world.

My dad used to share his success stories with me, and notably there were times when the stories were shut off like a faucet. I'd ask him, "How are sales?" and he'd reply, "Money is tight, Gary." I didn't really get that metaphor. How could something like dollar bills be tight or loose? I had heard about the ability to "stretch a dollar" but thinking of cash in terms of its flexibility never occurred to me.

Later, I'd learn that dad was onto something. The amount of money in circulation can change. By action of the Federal Reserve Board in the United States, the amount of available cash can be restricted or expanded. This can occur through raising or lowering interest rates and by manipulating the actual amount of currency that is printed and coined. So, in effect, money can be tight or loose. Additionally, when the economy shrinks, and companies spend less and less, job hunters and job creators can feel the pinch.

In a macroscopic, big-picture sense, there are diminished opportunities at large. And companies and people adopt a scarcity mentality. We come to think there isn't enough to go around. We tell ourselves there's not enough cash, not enough high-paying jobs or enough opportunities in general. By some measures, as I've just implied, this is an objective fact.

My dad was mostly in the advertising business, and he would follow that admission that money was tight with a positive statement. "Gary, in slow times, companies should advertise MORE, not less!" And of course, he was right. If it takes more effort to snare less leads and to close fewer deals, then that requires getting one's message before more eyes and more ears. You have to try harder to stay in the same place that you would be in "loose money" circumstances. We will return to this idea in a moment.

There is another argument I want to make to help you to find more appetizing opportunities in lean times. I'll say this very starkly: *there is never too little money to go around*. At any given time there are trillions of dollars available or in circulation in the economies of the world. I am speaking of deposits in checking and savings accounts, cash stuffed in people's mattresses and piggy banks, open credit lines on charge cards, and corporate credit lines to name just a few sources.

Additionally, there are assets in money market funds, dividends from stocks and other liquid resources that can be tapped. There are government grants, scholar-ships and fellowships, many of which are not even used because too few people apply for them. I could go on. Let me repeat, there's lots of cash. The only sticking point is that there isn't enough of it in your checking account. From the most superficial perspective, you are short on money. But that is not the underlying problem or chal-lenge. According to Robert Schuller, "You don't have a money problem. You have an *idea* problem."

Take a second and let that sink in. Ideas are the sources of wealth. Before there was a product like your smartphone, there was a smart idea that conceived of it. Ideas are where the value resides. Of course, by them-selves, they don't translate into cash. We need to "pro-ductize" these ideas, giving them form that people will pay value for.

Let me give you an example that pulls these ideas about scarcity and abundance, being cash-poor and idea-rich, all together. The seminar topic that really brought me initial fortune and fame was related to customer ser-vice. This subject did very well when the economy was doing reasonably well. But when money got tight, ser-vicing the clients became less of a priority. Getting new clients came to the fore as a more promising and pressing objective.

So, in sailing terms, I "tacked." I used the wind that was blowing me back to propel me forward. Instead of staying in the customer service area, I accentuated my sales training offerings. In lean times, selling became my lead topic. And once people bought that topic from me it was easy to get them to try the customer service topic, as well, as an add-on purchase. I made these shifts, repeatedly over the years, as the overall economy waxed and waned.

The *idea* of tacking, of using prevailing winds to propel me to profits irrespective of how or where they were blowing, was the breakthrough.

While it is objectively true in my experience that customer service becomes less of an in-demand topic in hard times, I didn't have to stay stuck in this scarcity thinking. "Where is the abundance, if it isn't in customer service?" became the question, for which, "In sales" became the reply.

This leads us to the thinking of the ancient Stoics. Epictetus said that it isn't events themselves that make us crazy. It is our interpretation of those events that does the trick. It isn't the low numbers we see in our checking account that are upsetting us. It is our interpretation that they must remain low, that there is no end to the scarcity we see, and that there are no alternatives we look to, that drive us to despair. We need to generate ideas that will help us to find the abundance that is hidden in the shroud of scarcity.

There are people growing rich in the severest recessions and depressions. I assure you they grew wealthy by looking for opportunities, confident that they exist, instead of staying mired in scarcity thinking.

Tip 20:
But Tell Me, Do You Like The Clothes?

I could tell you I always wanted to be a lawyer. I had the idea of dazzling a judge and jury with my incisive arguments, the drama of winning and losing, but hopefully winning much more than losing. But what really caught my eye were the ultra-cool three-piece suits TV and movie lawyers wore. Vests were a fashion item that should never have gone out of style. The concept of being able to take off your suit coat but then still have a formal "chest-plate," a gladiator's vestment, was the ultimate in sophistication, in my book. Today, my wardrobe doesn't contain a single three-piece suit, but it does have a lot of well-tailored double-breasted ensembles.

I was looking-up an old college and grad school chum, this morning. And I noticed he has a blog and portrays himself as a writer, toiling he says, over a keyboard for at least four hours a day. I never saw him this way, but I think he liked the clothes, especially the license to wear soft styled shoes, his signature item.

My theory is more folks than would admit choose what they do for a living based on the uniforms that go along with the job. If you want a high-paying job, you need to look the part. This doesn't mean you need to out-dress everyone else. You do need a keen sense of how you come across, sartorially. For instance, when I decided to pursue advanced college studies, and to teach at the college level, I grew my beard to fairly ample proportions. This was "dressing for success," in that atmosphere and it gave me an intellectual air.

When I changed my emphasis, moving into corporate consulting, the beard vanished, the moustache remained, until finally, that caterpillar crawled off my face. As a consultant, I was doing a significant program for a financial company. For eons, my uniform had been a navy blazer with grey slacks, a nice tie, and a white or light blue oxford shirt. Then, my client pulled me aside and he gave me a heads-up. He said suits were more suitable. Quickly, I bought some conservative pinstripes by an Italian designer, and that subject was never broached again. In fact, I became quite a fan of expensive, well-made suits. I would fly over to England during the Christmas holidays and load-up on a half-dozen at a time. This sounds excessive, but by that point I was spending a lot of time at financial firms. If you have ever seen the movie, "American Psycho," recall the scene where Christian Bale compares his business card to everyone else's in the room. They were all dressed as I dressed for my clients.

A mutual fund hired me to do an extensive and very lucrative consulting project. About thirteen years later, one of my trainees had moved over to a major insurance company, based in the Midwest. He suggested to the management that they bring me in to fix their customer service department, which I did. He recalled saying to the management, "Gary wore the most expensive suit I have ever seen." This may sound utterly superficial, but it wasn't a trivial detail. How I dressed announced success. And they needed to believe in my magic to invest in my work in the middle six-figures.

When I graduated from college I went to work for an upscale leasing company, located in Beverly Hills, California. One of my clients had two cars under lease: a Cadillac and a Chevy Wagon. The wagon had a lot of miles on it, so he needed a replacement. He specified he wanted a white wagon. Well, at that time I couldn't find one, but I said I did locate one in beige, which is close to white, sort of off-white. He approved the deal. I obtained the vehicle and he came in to switch out the old wheels for the new. But there was a problem.

He hated the color. I reiterated white wasn't available and this was the closest to it. He yelled back, "That isn't white. It's (Blank) yellow!" I asked him why the color is so important. "Look, my customers are farmers. I sell big sprinkler systems to them. And if they see me drive onto their farms in a rich car, they'll think I'm making too much money on them!" I tried to convince him the car was plain enough and they wouldn't get that impression. Finally, after a protracted silence, which led me to believe he was going to storm away in disgust, he relented and accepted the new car.

The moral to the story is he felt he knew his customers well and he very carefully orchestrated what they thought of him and his wealth. Part of his sales performance was the message his wheels sent to those buyers. He would never, ever drive up in his other ride, the Cadillac! In his case a car was not only a functional item, but something like a fashion accessory, just as a briefcase, a writing instrument, or even a suit of clothes. The other side of the coin is that we want wealth advisors to appear wealthy.

You will need to dress in a manner that is congruent with your occupation. If you hate wearing uniforms, don't go into nursing or medicine. Be willing to make adjustments, as I did with the facial hair changes and dropping the sport jacket and slacks for more formal suits. As you move up the income scale you may very well find that your style will be dictated by forces and traditions that you only marginally control. You may have to wear a suit or tie, but you'll get to choose which patterns you'll don on a given day.

If you completely abhor the idea that your adornments will be of an institution's choosing, then this could affect your income for better or for worse. Be mindful of this as you seek out that high-paying job. Dressing as you wish is a form of compensation, albeit a psychic one. Would you trade substantial dollars for the ability to work remotely in your pajamas? You may be faced with this decision. When I was being critiqued based on my navy and grey outfit, my immediate emotion was resentment. I got over that pretty quickly, when I started cashing my ample paychecks.

Tip 21:
Do Two Things At Once

I worked my way through college and grad school. I was completely on my own in the cold, cruel world, sob, sob. Mostly that's true, with a little drama added. No extra charge for that. "And why my struggles made me the person I am today!" So says the Horatio Alger version of my biography.

To go to college, I had to work. This meant accepting any job that could help me to pay for my first tiny apartment. That abode was a single room, a small bath, and a space across from my closet that contained a hot plate. That's where I did my cooking, and my cooking consisted of the occasional hamburger, nothing fancy. Not even sure if I had a fridge. I don't think so. The place was too small. But it was mine; all mine! That gave me a lot of satisfaction, and a modicum of privacy, as well.

Mostly my time was spent walking to work or to the bus to commute to school. At one point I worked the graveyard shift at Safeway supermarket, stocking shelves while Beethoven's 9th symphony blasted though the giant store. My co-workers on that odd shift were eccentric, to say the least. Later, in college, I'd take a Music Appreciation course, and as you can imagine, I nailed the Beethoven unit. You never know when or where your exposures to these things will take you.

What I can say is this, which I believe you'll find in your career. It is easier to do two things at once, than doing things one at a time. School plus work was a great combination for me. Of course, the end of every day, or night, brought exhaustion. At least I had no trouble falling asleep!

Here is something that I learned. When you do two seemingly different things, one of them makes the other all that more enjoyable. School could be a pain, with all of the homework and such. But when my classes ended and my job began, I was in a totally different culture. For one thing, I was being paid. And my diligence on the job could bring me rapid raises and promotions. Comparatively, it was going to take years to earn the degrees that I was pursuing in school.

On the other hand, business can be tedious, too. Peter F. Drucker, the management sage I studied with actually remarked, "Well-run businesses are boring." The aim of most enterprises is to duplicate success. And the way to do that is to develop and to deploy "rational routines." They may be bringing in the bucks, but routines, by definition are boring.

When I would get bored at the job, there was usually something going on with school to create some excitement like the arrival of a hot band for our free open-air assemblies. In other words, when one activity gets you down, the other can pick you up. Emotionally, all of your eggs are not in the same basket. And sometimes, there are cool synergies that weave together and make both endeavors more successful.

For instance, when I was the sales manager at Time-Life, I noticed that I would introduce a new procedure and it wasn't implemented right away. I'd leave the room, and a group discussion ensued where the "old timer," the most seasoned sales rep seemed to run the conversation.

In my authoritarian sensibility, I figured I'd announce a plan and instantly, it would be put into practice. Of course, that's not how organizational change occurs. Luckily, I was studying Sociology and learning about working groups, and how informal leaders held sway over productivity, even more than people like me with titles and supervisorial responsibilities. When there were conflicts between informal leaders and formal leaders on policies or procedures, and particularly on workflow and achievement, guess who "won?" The famous "Hawthorne Studies" at Western Electric that we studied in class suggested on many matters informal leaders like the old timer I mentioned, were far more influential than formal leaders wanted to acknowledge. This wisdom helped me to change my approach.

Bud, who was the informal leader in the sales group, was the top producer. When the management spot that I earned came up, he and I were in contention for it. I won, and he lost. He felt bitter, and in ways large and small I came to feel he was sabotaging my leadership hoping that I would fail, and he would replace me. My Sociology studies taught me to pay attention to small group dynamics. My team became my laboratory, and I learned a ton. After trying to get him to come into the light and help the team, Bud refused. His negativity overflowed and I had to let him go.

I was 19 at the time, and this was my first management position, and it was a challenging one. This was my first crisis. After letting Bud go, I spoke to my New York boss, who called in nightly for sales figures. I explained what happened, saying Bud had to go; there was no other choice. He replied, "Well, I hope you're right!" I was. Our productivity surged after we saw the last of him.

What is important for our purpose is to appreciate that my college work fit perfectly with my work-work. Not only was it easier to do two things at once. It was more productive. One didn't take away from the other. Together the two meant more than one plus one, it was more like four.

I suppose at the margins if I had all the time in the world to study and if I didn't have to work, my grades might have been slightly higher. Or if I had worked exclusively, I might have brought in more bucks in the short term. But in the long term I'm grateful I stretched. As it would turn out, I went on to have both business and academics careers. And of course, I found a way to have them, simultaneously!

The two things you do, or perhaps even more than two, don't have to be work and school, though they were a good fit for me. They can be work and more work; two different jobs. But the emphasis is on "different." That way, one can be a form of relief from the next, and you're likely to learn more.

Tip 22:
Think Like An Entrepreneur

A short while ago I wrote a book and recorded an audio titled, *The 40+ Entrepreneur*. In it, I detail some strategies that were first articulated by my professor and mentor, management sage Peter. F. Ducker. These apply to finding opportunities and to adopting a competitive strategy.

You need to think like an entrepreneur even if you are a job hunter, and especially if you are looking to create a new, high-paying job. Seven sources of change can guide you to spot high-paying job opportunities. They are:

- The unexpected
- Incongruity
- Process need
- Change in industry or market structure
- Demographics
- Changes in perception
- New knowledge

Let's start with the **unexpected**. The first opportunity is the unexpected success. I will speak from my experience in titling books. I have a good sense of which titles will capture the imagination of readers and audio listeners. When I have a strong hunch about one I am eager to share it with my agent who in turn discusses it with my publishers. At that stage some of these wonderful ideas never take another breath. They are politely opposed, and I have so many ideas that I don't usually have time to fight losing causes. I'll abandon them and go on to the next one.

Occasionally, I have doubts about my own titles, though I still write them with enthusiasm and authority. Many of these go on to become "sleepers." They are unexpected successes, taking on lives of their own. In some cases, the material they contain resonates so intensely that I simply must do more with them.

A book needs to become an audiobook. And that begs to become a seminar and a keynote speech, and possibly a continuing education offering at a university. I have to avoid overlooking the title's success simply because I didn't believe enough in its potential, at one point. Dismissing it precisely because its success seems accidental is the wrong thing to do.

When it comes to ideas, strategies, and jobs, we need to "Feed the winners, and starve the losers." There are companies, such as IBM that achieved astonishing success in building large computers. When PCs came along, people in that company resisted the idea of making them because "Mainframes built this place." Those folks were defending the past. They were reluctant to seize the unexpected success of Apple, for instance, as an opportunity as machines became smaller and smaller.

Likewise, let's say you are strong in a given area. You may not realize the gift because your skill comes to you so easily as to be thought of as insignificant. You could believe, falsely, that anything worthwhile must entail struggle and great sacrifice. But "naturals" in almost every field do not struggle at all. Great mathematicians and composers "intuit" their fields in the same way that a dream pointed Einstein to Relativity Theory. If you're suffering, something is wrong.

I spent a day with an insurance salesperson in Southwest Florida. We went on cold calls, visiting offices unannounced in the hope that an executives and small business owners might like to chat about coverage. Door-to-door selling is anathema to most folks. It's like that nightmare that you're walking to school and suddenly you notice you're naked. I would guess 99.99% of the entire population would rate this activity toward the bottom of their list of best occupations. It might even be lower than snake rustling.

But this gentleman whom I accompanied seemed to thrive on it. He wasn't reluctant or ruffled in the least. Financially, he did quite well. Having this gift means he could sell anything, including items and services that would pay him far more than selling insurance. He doesn't see his own strength in perspective. He simply doesn't appreciate its earning power. Therefore, know your strengths and seize unexpected successes.

The second source of opportunity is from **spotting incongruities**.

I did this when I noticed companies were complaining about high fuel prices. Specifically, it cost more and more to deploy their field sales forces, paying for gas and lodging and airfares. When I offered my first workshop in California on the topic of Telephone Effectiveness, I didn't exploit this incongruity between the way things always were when it came to budgeting sales costs, and the way in which they had suddenly become; far more expensive. But when I offered the next session of the program about three months later, I tapped this theme. I said "Beat the high cost of fuel by using the phone, instead."

That appeal acknowledged something mighty and critical had changed, and I was offering a viable means with which to cope. Sometimes there are income incongruities that you can exploit. A few years ago, when the oil fields of the Dakotas were gushing, an economic boom was heard around the country. The unemployment rate in most of the land was around 10% and only 3% in North Dakota. McDonald's was reportedly paying workers there twice as much as it paid in other places. There were numerous people that ventured north from places like Texas to work in the oil industry. They lived in temporary "Man Camps," no frills barracks and trailers. And they sent home and banked a ton of money, which they were able to accumulate.

The story changed later, when oil prices bottomed. But similar tales are being told today, in places such as San Francisco, where the technology sector is in a boom cycle.

A third source of opportunity is the **process need**. Companies need sales to sustain operations and build profits. Sales come from leads; people that have a need, believe the need is important, and are willing to pay to have someone else satisfy it.

The sales process entails pursuing leads to a purchasing conclusion. There is what I call, "The math of success." For instance, it could take the average company five to ten leads to create one sale. After they have been in business for a while firms know what this ratio is and they can confidently compute how much money they'll have to invest in leads to earn new business. But sometimes this ratio gets out of whack. Instead of leads costing $100 each, they soar to $500 each or even more. These firms now have an urgent process need.

They can address it several ways, and someone like us can help them and justify earning a premium wage for doing so. For example, this very thing has happened to firms that are alternative lenders. They make short-term cash advances to companies that would not qualify for traditional bank financing. Lenders get most of their leads from Internet advertising. But they are increasingly weak opportunities that are sold, simultaneously, to a dozen or more lenders. This creates a "calling frenzy," in which the leads are preyed on by a dozen vendors at once, all of them making big promises.

Exclusive leads, where a company is only going to speak to one source, are vastly superior and generally are the most expensive leads to buy. Remember that insurance seller that is so comfortable walking into businesses? Matching his strength to the opportunity to provide alternative lenders with leads would be a natural fit. On average, he might be able to find two to three companies in need, each day. If he could train others to do what he does, he could develop a team to build leads.

If alternative lenders on average earn $4,000 from a sale, how much of that would they be willing to invest solid leads? The answer is more than you think. Each sale carries with it the likelihood that the new client will return for a second loan, also worth $4,000. So, you or someone else can serve this process need for leads, at a profit.

There are other ways to address the challenge of soaring lead costs. One of them is to train sellers to compete more effectively with the 11 rivals that will be phoning their current lead sources. If sellers can enhance their techniques by merely 10 percent, they'll close more deals at a lower overall cost.

Changes in an industry or market structure can be devastating, but like the Chinese symbol for crisis, there are also opportunities.

The insurance industry is shifting from an agent-driven to an Internet driven marketing structure. More people are abandoning traditional brick and mortar agencies in favor of providers like Progressive and Esurance. The good news is the cost to consumers for their auto and home coverage may decline. But for the agents that are losing their book of business, as it is called, this change is ominous.

They have to adapt, giving clients good reasons to favor the human touch over the cold computer click. Those that figure out how to do it, investing in customer relationships, can be big winners, financially. If you have good people skills, insurance sales may actually be a career to explore because there will always be incentives and room for those that can put business on the books, while helping customers remain loyal.

Another source of change that can provide great opportunities is **demographics**. Because populations in developed countries are aging, there are more jobs available servicing senior citizens at a profit. I detail this and the other opportunities in my book and audio, *The 40+ Entrepreneur.*

One of the less obvious facts is that people are interested in working longer because they are staying healthy longer. This means they have time to open businesses, return to school, and to work in occupations that serve their older age cohort, for instance providing care and companionship to the infirm. Some of my home health care clients are reporting a boom in their businesses. In some cases, they cannot keep up with demand. And that demand is being subsidized in many cases by the government through programs such as Medicare.

Changes in perception and meaning are also sources of opportunity. Today's headlines are filled with items about radical religious groups that want to impose their beliefs on others, often cruelly. This radicalism is making many people rethink their own beliefs.

There is a growing cohort of folks that consider themselves non-believers, altogether. They don't have a church, synagogue, or mosque to attend. And they're feeling left out of the mainstream. Finding ways to provide meaning to these individuals is a great opportunity. It could be through the development of associations, businesses, recreational opportunities such as tours, and even mating and dating web sites. Wherever people are under-served, there are opportunities.

Finally, **new knowledge** is an entrepreneurial opportunity. Recently the human genome has become better understood, and genetic testing of many kinds is being done. This is mainly to detect problems and to remedy them, but there are also nascent opportunities to profit from such breakthroughs.

Currently, there are companies that will analyze your DNA and tell you about your biological ancestry and heritage. The cost at present is a few hundred dollars, but this is sure to drop as competitors enter the picture. Lots of folks, perhaps numbering in the millions, are thrilled to hear that 70% of their ancestry can be traced to one continent or to one specific region. It is certainly fun for them to discuss at family parties!

Our tendency is to be change resistant, but each of the opportunities I have pointed to here, for earning higher pay, actually exploit change. Notice these changes and ask what is it about them that I can use to create a high paying job? You may surprise yourself with the number of opportunities you uncover.

Tip 23:
Do You Have A Money Personality?

I find myself purposely telling the same story, again and again. It symbolizes many things, but for our purpose it asks a fundamental question: What are *you* willing to do to create a high-paying job?

Here is one person's answer. I was consulting for a financial company in Houston, Texas. Their goal was to sell government guaranteed bond funds to institutional investors. Their clients included universities, major banks, pension funds, and other entities that sought an above average return on investment, with minimal or no risk.

Because lots of money was involved, this meant most sales took a while to consummate, between 30 and 90 days, on average. The salespeople were paid on a straight-commission basis, which I mentioned earlier. What this means, to put it in dramatic but realistic terms, is when they sell, they eat. And when they don't, who knows? Somehow they have to get by to live to sell another day. Most sellers were reasonably thick-skinned, having sold investments before. The typical recruit earned his or her first sale within 30–60 days. That would be typical. Now I am going to profile someone that did not fit that typical mold.

Stewart did not come across as the smartest seller on earth. He was more of a plodder in speech, but don't get me wrong. He wasn't mentally challenged. He just came across differently. Maybe it was telephone communication that handicapped him. In person, he was likeable and mild-mannered, very polite, in fact. I found him a good person to work with. How long did it take him to taste his first victory?

The answer is longer than anyone imagined. He did not get his first order until he had been on the job for a full ten months. He suffered through more than 300 punishing days of nothingness. Some seemed close to buying, but no one took the leap. And yet he found the strength to soldier on.

Let me ask you. How long could you last without a paycheck: A week, two, three or four? Possibly a month or two if others were supporting you? He went for ten months! Can you imagine the "social pain" he must have endured? Others, including those that hired-on after he did, earned sales and "rang the bell" as they were encouraged to do when they scored. His bell was ominously silent.

How much more out of place can you feel when you are an experienced seller that doesn't seem able to sell? Imagine being his significant other. He comes home and you ask, "How did you do, today?" What could he say? After even a month of zero results the same sad song would probably produce stoic resignation at best, and wonderment about his sanity. And yet he soldiered on.

Some years ago I came across a very helpful book, written by Dr. Sidney Lecker, a psychoanalyst. Now out of print, *The Money Personality* says certain types of folks create and sustain wealth far better than others. Stewart was one of these folks. Where 99% of people would have found his non-results humiliating and too painful to bear, he saw his non-success as a price that had to be paid. No matter how long it took, he was going to hang in there until the tide turned in his favor. And turn it did.

After ten months he got his first commission, and let me tell you, it was a whopper! He earned one million dollars from that initial deal. There are 4.3 weeks in a month. If he toiled for 40 hours a week times 4.3 weeks, he invested 172 hours a month, or 1,720 hours during his ten months of "starvation." He earned about $582.00 per hour, when you break it down. That's right up there with top lawyers and other first-class professionals. It is not the same pay politicians can command when they deliver speeches, which can run into the hundreds of thousands of dollar per hour, each. Still, Stewart's terrible non-paying job was transformed through that initial sale into a high-paying job, wouldn't you agree?

It is legitimate to ask this question: What was he being compensated for? On what basis did he deserve a million-dollar payday? I have already told you he was not a gifted or outstanding salesperson, though he did have some experience. He earned his million because he cultivated and deployed a money personality. The specific traits he exhibited were these.

His *persistence* was off the charts. He kept repeating his sales routine, no matter what.

He was *insensitive* to the opinions of others around him. Most of us think that our sensitivity is a measure of our desirability as human beings. But in business, it can be precisely the opposite that brings substantially above average income. Money personalities are insensitive to, and actually when necessary, they are resistant to the opinions of spectators in the grandstands. "But what are my sales-mates thinking about me right now as I fail so conspicuously?" This is precisely the wrong type of concern to have. Money personalities know who is paying their way. It is not their fellow salespeople; it is customers. Anything that distracts them from this realization and the amazing focus it brings, is an expensive and potentially devastating distraction.

Money personalities *don't let secondary gains replace primary gains.* Being popular, getting the approval and respect of irrelevant people, all of these things feel good but they are like cotton candy. The taste good, temporarily, but they cannot be replacements for solid nutrients. You must remember you are seeking to create a high-paying job. That is your primary aim. Therefore, *money* is the number one goal; let's not quibble about that.

Annually, there are surveys done that appear in the *Wall Street Journal* and other publications. They report what people say is important in a job. Repeatedly, "money" is ranked somewhere around third on the list. This fact is touted by lots of people as "proof" people are motivated by other, higher and nobler motives. That's a lot of bull. Survey takers don't want to appear greedy or preoccupied with earning the "almighty dollar" because it seems base and crass and beneath them. They are being dishonest in sharing their true feelings because they are more concerned about being negatively judged than they are interested in honestly stating money making is important to them.

Money personalities "suffer no guilt" about true motivations, and they keep first things first, says Dr. Lecker. You should, too.

Be persistent in pursuing your goal. Resist the influence of others that would distract you from reaching it. And don't let secondary gains displace your primary gains.

This is the price you pay to create a high-paying job.

Tip 24:
Don't Compare Yourself to Others

In traffic, when you are barely making headway on a road that has parallel lanes, it is really stupid to change lanes incessantly from one to the other. Yet my passengers always prod me to do this. Suddenly, the lane to your right or left starts advancing, and a car you passed a few minutes before has now darted ahead of you. Well, that's completely unacceptable! Your competitive juices simply don't want to let that go, the fact that this laggard is now a frontrunner and he will arrive at his destination possibly a minute or more before you get to yours.

If you look at the logic of my last sentence, you will begin to appreciate how dumb it is to peg your progress to his or hers. "He will arrive at his destination," and "You will get to yours." I said to my passengers. That's an important point. You are going to two different places. You are not really in a race, expected to cross the same finishing line. You started out at different entry points. And yet, based on simply being side by side on the road for a while we instantly behave as if we are in a competition.

Taken to the extreme, emotions can get heated, resulting in our making impulsive cuts into traffic that expose us and others to grave bodily harm and even to the possibility of death. Plus, there is always the possibility that two drivers will lock horns in competitive mode and will road-rage, dangerously confronting each other. This needless activity, mental, physical, and vehicular has the precise impact of slowing down traffic, overall. I call it "Competing for a single car-length." Believe me when I tell you I've done it. And I have to resist the impulse to do it again.

As you pursue the goal of creating a high-paying job try to avoid comparing your progress to others. They aren't heading the same place, either. And if it were really a race, you would have started out at two very different points. I spent most of my youth in an affluent city. My friends' parents were in show business, the arts, and the professions. Comparatively, my family felt "poor." Looking back, I can see some objective evidence for this memory, but as a mature person, I also see that any self-pity I felt was stupid. Affluence is a relative construct. In the world at the time there were billions of people that fared worse than we did, but they weren't my reference group. That group consisted of kids whose folks sent them to Europe for a year of carefree travel before they entered college, or they cannily figured out a way for the year to be packaged with college credits.

At around age 18, I had to go to work, to support myself as I trekked to a community college and job sites on the bus. Though I told myself I was building character as I faced these challenges, on another level I couldn't help comparing my progress to that of my peers. They were handed fancy new cars or very spiffy used ones. They had money for fun and frivolity. Even when I was able to get a few extra bucks in my hands, who had the time to dawdle?

I purposely donned a different mindset. I told myself I needed to "Think like someone new to this country." I had to accept that in many ways I was starting at the bottom of the ladder. I didn't stay there all that long. Developing sales skills which I describe elsewhere, I was able to earn above-average money for a college student. What progress did that peer group of mine make? Some of them "bummed around" for more than a year after high school. Others dropped in and out of college, as the spirit moved them. A few demonstrated a strong work ethic and went on to graduate and professional schools. Others joined family businesses, where any shortcomings could be buffered by the contributions of parents and siblings.

At our first ten-year reunion, I was already a tenure-track college professor with a Ph.D. at a prestigious liberal arts university. This fact nearly put me in a class by myself. I would go on to write best-selling books, become a media commentator, launch a successful international consulting and keynote speaking practice, and more.

Flash forward to today. I am still producing a prodigious number of books, audios, and seminars. The only person I'm competing with is myself. I am trying to beat yesterday, not someone else. It is all too easy to succumb to the illusion that life is a contest, the purpose of which is to win, to beat everyone else. I believe the reason I was able to create a succession of high-paying jobs is precisely because I started to ignore the progress my peer group was making.

On some level I appreciated that we started out at different points. In some cases they were the proverbial folks that were "Born on third base and were told they hit a triple." With an entitlement mindset, surrounded by indulgent relatives and not motivated by a sense of deficiency, they were to encounter a huge shock: that they weren't as talented or as destined for easy victories as they may have thought.

I came to appreciate everything. My first very used car, a VW bug with a zillion miles on it, was the sweetest ride in the world. I earned it by snaring my community college's student leadership scholarship. My first apartment was a shoebox with four walls and a hot plate for cooking. But I made the most satisfying burgers in the world there. Ultimately, I have out-earned and out-achieved many if not all of those high school pals and acquaintances. I did it, mainly, by not competing for car lengths.

Don't compare your career progress to anybody else's. Don't succumb to the awful emotion of contempt, which Aristotle defined as that emotion we feel when we witness others getting something we are not getting.

Let their victories be theirs, and let your victories be yours.

Tip 25:
The Highest Paid People Command Attention

I can't tell you how many patents are filed each year in the United States alone, but it is a huge number. And it is ditto for other countries. Of all of those new and improved gizmos, how many ever get into production? Frightfully few, is the answer.

When I was growing up I was introduced to a fellow named Red McCarthy, who had been a championship figure skater. Red was in retirement, but oh was he busy! In his garage he had built a home gym. It had a system of pulleys that enable the user to work on all the major muscle groups. Red predicted it would change the world, and he promoted it, tirelessly. But I inferred that his device, as cool and helpful and advanced as it was never found the right resources it took to succeed.

In my garage I have free weights and an exercise machine or two. They are very similar to the device Red labored on for those years, in obscurity. He wasn't really that far ahead of his time, though I do believe he foresaw the fitness revolution that would catch on with consumers.

If there was a failure of calibration, of timing, it was the inability to get the right sort of attention paid to what he was achieving, by the right people with the right resources. The operative term in the last sentence isn't "resources." Traditional wisdom says "money makes money" and most new business ideas fail because of a lack of capitalization. I don't agree.

Businesses and people that want to create high paying jobs for themselves fail because *they garner inadequate attention.* In other words, *they don't get noticed.* I mention elsewhere if you look for jobs where everyone else is looking, say at online employment boards, you will be competing with hordes of individuals. Try getting noticed and standing out if you look like and sound like and seem like every other animal in the herd.

Possibly the fastest or the luckiest cow is the one that is in front of the stampede and arrives first at the Human Resources department gate. That person might receive a tiny advantage and be conspicuous. Perhaps within moments and certainly days, that first cow will be merged into the herd, and his distinguishing marks will blend in with everyone else's, making him disappear into a sea of camouflage. Today, more than ever, we are all swimming in a sea of lookalikes. The Internet provides so many apparent choices for everything, products, services, and people, that becoming distinctive is the highest paid attribute anyone can have.

Let me give you an example. One of my coaching clients is transforming himself into a consultant. He works in the software field and has identified a rapidly growing niche that he'd like to exploit. Upon researching this opportunity, we were simply blown away by the type and quality of competition out there from every corner of the universe. Large companies and small ones were rushing to join this stampede. His very pertinent challenge became, "How do I differentiate myself?" This is pretty much identical to asking, "How can I stand out."

Basically, there are two choices. He can become "smaller" than they are, focusing his attention on and developing expertise in a sub-unit of this burgeoning topic. Ideally, it would be an area that is disproportionately significant, yet it is overlooked by seemingly everyone else. On the competitive battlefield it would be a tiny peak on a molehill that he could occupy and defend.

The other approach is to become larger. Just as we felt overwhelmed by the sheer number of available consultants, it is assured that buyers of their consulting services would share our feeling. They would benefit from being able to better evaluate and distinguish the most useful and cost effective providers. So, his consultancy could position him as a gatekeeper. "Come to me and I'll help you to select the best consultant for you." He might decide to not charge the customer for this service. Instead, he would be compensated a brokerage fee from the consultant that won the assignment.

This is the same pay structure as travel agents used (remember them?) and the remaining ones continue to use. If you book your voyage through them, they are paid by the cruise line and not by you. If you book directly with the cruise line, you'll pay the same price.

As an attorney, if I have a client come to me with a matter that I cannot completely manage on my own, with the blessing of the client I'll refer the person to someone that is better suited to help. There are also some clients that have an existing representative but find communicating with that person difficult, so they retain me to intermediate.

Let's say you are going to become a "gatekeeper" consultant. How could you stand out and get the attention needed to build your practice? You could write articles and news releases that have these headlines: "How To Avoid Hiring The Wrong Consultant" and "5 Danger Signs To Notice Before Hiring A Consultant" and "Stop Hiring Before Reading This Warning!" These seem like negative themes, don't they? There is an attention-getting reason for that. In another section we already spoke about how people are more motivated by the fear of loss than by the prospect of gain. Earning $500 is far less powerful a motivation to people than not losing $500.

You've heard the expression, "There is no such thing as 'bad' publicity." What does this mean? Keeping your name in front of an audience is a paramount objective, even if the context in which they come across it is less than completely favorable. Writing great publicity and effective self-promotion operate on the premise that the sharp angle, the "difference that makes a difference" in your positioning will lead you to being repeatedly noticed.

That is the precursor to creating a high-paying job and qualifying for raises, promotions and far better opportunities after that. Remember this headline: The Highest Paid People Command Attention.

Tip 26: Negotiate Your Time Commitments

When I was in the student employment office at my college campus I peered over the shoulder of a guy presenting a stack of flyers to the clerk.

They read:

> WANTED: BRIGHT, ARTICULATE STUDENTS
>
> EARN FULL-TIME PAY FOR PART-TIME WORK!

That message certainly got my attention, and I blurted out, "That's me!"

With a wide grin the gentleman advertising the job asked me to tell him a little about myself. Two minutes later, we agreed to meet that afternoon for an interview. I started that night and earned my first sale. The company, Time-Life Books, changed my life. It not only lived up to the promise of the flyer, but it provided me with invaluable experience in selling and management. I would cash-in on what I learned for years to come, starting my own consulting practice and selling my unique seminars to 35 universities, largely based on the skills I learned at Time-Life.

Remembering that flyer, for years I thought the most attention getting words were, "Bright, Articulate Students." It was rare, and still is, for companies to say they are recruiting smart people. That came as a relief to me. I was tired of dumb jobs, bagging groceries and stocking shelves, delivering fish in the sweltering summer heat. But for our purposes, we're going to focus on the second line of that flyer because it provides a hint as to what you should always be seeking to do:

EARN FULL-TIME PAY FOR PART-TIME WORK!

The title of this project as you know is *How to Create Your Own High-Paying Job.* And by high-paying a typical interpretation would be finding or developing a job that paid more than other jobs. But this isn't the only way to define, high-paying. An important question is to ask and then to re-ask, "How much time am I being required to put in for the amount of money I take out?"

Let me give you an example of how you can change this configuration for the better and dramatically increase the payback you get for the time you invest. I was doing an extended project for a financial company in the Southeast. This required me to travel, weekly, coast to coast. Part of this drill was enjoyable. Because I flew so often, I was regularly upgraded to Business Class on the Boeing 777 that transported me from Los Angeles to Miami. If you have to spend so much time on the road as I did, it's nice to do it as luxuriously as possible, and the 777 was the way to go. I could kick back or get work done, or both.

My clients paid for economy class airfares, so as far as that expense was concerned, it was contained. Still, weekly travel presented them with a big tab. The president of the firm asked me what we could do to trim this expense. Pay close attention, because this is a way you, too, can turn lemons into lemonade and boost your earnings.

My first response was negative, defensive. "Why are they trying to cut me back when my program is so successful?" But then I asked myself how I could transform what seemed to be a step backwards into a giant step forward. Typically, my training day consisted of about two and a half hours in the morning session and the same amount of time in the afternoon. There were about 5 contact hours. By spreading this time over the day, this schedule enabled my trainees to get some work done before we assembled at 9:30 and after we adjourned, at 3:30. It also enabled me to pace myself a little bit. Training or public speaking is fun and energizing but it takes a toll. And when you factor in some jet lag from the commuting, I have always been mindful about staving-off exhaustion.

Here's what I worked out. We had scheduled about 20 additional weeks at that point. I offered to do the balance of the program in 10 weeks.

The ordinary way to accomplish this would be to double-up on the number of trainees in each seminar. If we usually had 7, we'd take on 14. However, doing this was not wise, because there is much less commitment shown by trainees when they are in larger groups. So, you are "processing" them faster, but their learning and application of the knowledge decrease, significantly. It's a pennywise but pound-foolish way to economize, especially on travel.

I suggested this alternative: I would do the remaining 20 weeks of training in 10 weeks by scheduling two classes per day instead of one. This meant I had to put in a 10-hour training day, instead of 5 hours. I would be paid at the original contract price and this meant I would double my pay for each day.

Surely, this would take more energy to do on my part. I would be more fatigued at the end of each week. This could impact my leisure time by zapping the energy I could channel into other things.

Then again, by sandwiching two events into the same day I was able to double my *daily* rate of pay. This is significant. By doing so, I freed my calendar of ten entire weeks, which I ended up selling to another major company.

Time is the ultimate perishable. We have a limited number of clock hours. When you can negotiate the same rate of pay, but agree to get the work done faster, freeing up your calendar, you have given yourself a big spike in income.

Mine is a dramatic example. Another way to accomplish this result is by scheduling certain working tasks for what one of my business contacts labeled as, "garbage time." These are off-hours that generally give you no income. We're speaking of TV time that you might waste pasted to a screen that you can monetize and be paid for. Especially if you work remotely, assigning income-producing activities to garbage time frees up your "primetime" to do other things. You can add another job, part-time or full, or simply get errands done.

Changing the clock can occur in other ways. Given my distance to the city, which can run to two hours in traffic, if I can start at a client's site at 6:00 or 7:00 in the morning and knock-off by noon, I have actually recovered a lot of time. This means I can commute during light traffic. This easily saves two hours and sometimes three hours a day and it makes driving pleasurable. Moreover, it limits the wear and tear on my brakes, and it improves my gas mileage. These are all compensations.

Business owners are always seeking ways to get more done with less. That's called productivity. Likewise, when you are selling your labor, you need to do the same. If you can double a day's output by using basically the same inputs, you can double your income on the spot.

This can transform an okay job into a high-paying one. Or it can make an otherwise good job into an outstanding one. Regularly ask yourself, how can I re-negotiate my time commitments?

Tip 27:
And Why Should We Hire YOU?

In the old world, it wasn't know-how that found you work. It was "know-who," your family, school, and business connections. Even if you weren't the sharpest blade in the shed, the fastest horse in the race, or the cutest of other clichés, you could find work and create a relatively high-paying job for yourself. You could simply ask around. "Know anybody that is hiring?"

Today, we have thousands of social media "connections" which are supposed to expand on the family contacts and other ties of old. Unfortunately, they are often tapped in a way that is very inadequate.

I recently received this note along with a resume from a new contact at LinkedIn: *"Greetings. Thank you for connecting. Now I am looking for a better job. Request you to forward my CV to any of the openings you know. Thank you. Have a great day."*

I don't fault this person for reaching out or for trying, quite the opposite. However, this note is woefully inadequate on many grounds. The major fault is it doesn't address the pivotal questions:

What type of job opportunity is he looking for? What are his strengths? What is his pertinent experience? What is his target employment market? Where does he want to locate? Why did he choose me to help, what do I bring to the party? Why should I help him? What's in it for me?

What this person is doing is asking me to either assume the answers to these queries or to go by the seat of my pants and simply and robotically email everyone I know that has an opening. Do you realize how preposterous this request is? And can you guess how much it is doomed to fail? I don't know him at all but I am being called on to recommend him.

In a way I have done something similar. As a college professor, a corporate consultant, and a career coach I come into brief contact with lots of folks. Some ask for a reference. Typically, I have had some first-hand communication, some experience with them. I can set aside time, in a few cases where I suspect I can help, to learn more about them. Then I might feel comfortable putting my credibility on the line by recommending them.

But let's back-up. Everyone is a stranger before becoming an acquaintance or a friend. If we dealt only with people we already know, we' would hardly expand our circle of contacts. The trick is to build bridges, efficiently. The way this happens is through effective communication. Albert Einstein said, "If you can't explain something simply, you don't understand it well enough."

The person who emailed me that note does not know the answers to the above-noted questions well enough. That is the starting point to any contact you are going to make, someone from whom you will request assistance.

Let's review these questions:

What type of job opportunity are you looking for?
"I'll do anything!" is probably not the right answer unless you have zero employment experience or credentials, and you are looking for an unpaid internship or minimum wage job.

What are your strengths?
This includes interpersonal strengths. "I find a way to get along with everyone because I like people and I'm a good listener."

What is your pertinent experience?
"I've been a sales manager for five years with a great track record of increasing and sustaining sales in different economic circumstances."

What is your target employment market?
"I'm interested in joining a new company that needs sales right away."

Where do you want to be located?
"Though I live in Channel Islands, I'm willing to relocate for the right opportunity."

Why did you choose me to help, what do I bring to the party?
"You are a respected professor, consultant and best-selling author, and if you can recommend me it will carry a lot of weight."

Why should I help him? What's in it for me?
"I'll make you proud. When I'm in a position to reciprocate, believe me, I will be happy to do so."

I suppose, gazing back on these questions, we could boil them down to two, if necessary:

Why you?

Why me?

These need to be addressed in the same way companies compose and communicate a USP, a Unique Sales Proposition. Their offers to customers need to get attention and then stand out from the crowd. So do yours.

Harking back to that email I received, is there anything that person wrote that says he or she is worth my attention and is unique? Why should *anyone* hire this individual? I'm sure there are positive replies to this question that can support a job search. What are they?

I have found it helpful to use what I call the PEP format to explain why they should hire you. This is a communication tool that can be used in an email or in a talk over the phone or in a face-to-face job interview. I explain it in detail in my book *"Crystal Clear Communication: How to Explain Anything Clearly in Speech or Writing."*

There are three parts, each following the next:

POINT: You state a point, such as "You should hire me."

EVIDENCE: You support that point with three specific reasons or forms of evidence.

POINT: You restate the point. "So, for these reasons you should hire me."

Your answer to those questions I introduced earlier can supply the three reasons you will supply under EVIDENCE.

For example, you could say: First, I am an effective communicator. I find a way to get along with everyone because I like people and I'm a good listener. Second, I'm qualified. I've been a sales manager for five years with a great track record of increasing and sustaining sales in different economic circumstances. And third, I'll make you proud. I aim to succeed!"

Then you restate your point:

POINT: "So, for these reasons you should hire me."

I'm using the "should" word on purpose because I am persuading. One of the strengths of the PEP format is that you can use it simply to inform or to instruct.

POINT: "If you look at my career, you'll see three significant themes." Then, you simply explain them. Especially if you want to create a high-paying job you need to address the overarching question every hiring authority will need to hear: "And why should we hire YOU?"

Remember what Einstein said. If you cannot articulate the answer to this simply, you don't understand the reasons well enough, yourself.

The good news is if you can organize and present even a barely passable answer, but in a supremely organized way using PEP, you can gain an advantage that will make that job yours.

Tip 28:
Don't Be Tom Sawyered

I was doing a national training project for an airline. Two of their managers sat down to have lunch with me before the meeting got underway. The purpose was to calibrate our goals and for me to hear a description of the sales team that I would be improving. At one point, one of my contacts said, "These people are so much fun if the company didn't pay me, I'd pay them just to watch!" Of course, this was a giddy exaggeration, and by "fun" I came to believe he was saying his associates were "bizarre." Was he serious? Would he pay to watch? Of course not, and yet today this is what some companies are actually trying to pull off.

It is a riff on that old theme Mark Twain exposed through one of his best-known characters, Tom Sawyer. You may recall, Tom was tasked by Auntie to whitewash her fence. Tom didn't want to do it, so being the clever lad he was, he "allowed" his buddies to do it for him. He characterized the task as fun and important and not something that just anybody could be permitted to do. Indeed, Tom was so over the top in building up the benefits of painting Auntie's fence that he charged his pals for the privilege of doing it.

As readers, you may remember how you felt as Mark Twain presented this case study of a budding con man in action. I think I snickered because he was snookering his friends that way. Never, ever would I fall for that line of bull, right?

Yet to some extent I am sure I have fallen for it when companies have sold me on what a privilege it is to be chosen to associate with them. The appeal almost always comes down to this offer, phased in various ways: "If you want to be a part of our team you need to know we don't pay the retail rate for anything. It's just not in the corporate DNA. So, you'll need to cut your fee by at least (50%), otherwise our purchasing and legal folks will kick this proposal out."

Here's another way they whittle you down: "You do know, of course, that having our company on your resume does wonders for your career. It's going to get you into doors that would otherwise be closed and the net effect could mean hundreds of thousands and even millions of dollars over the course of your career. But you'll need to do something for us . . ."

Largely, my approach has been to counter these cons by saying: "I treasure all of my clients, and it's just assumed that my previous consulting clients will help me to earn future business, providing I have lived up to expectations, which I will do. So, the value I get is just a fraction of the value I confer, and I'm sure you can afford to pay my modest fees, can't you?"

They have stated the obvious: I do want to associate with them because they are successful and well regarded. In return, I say that I work with successful firms for precisely the reason they can afford to pay me and their business will lead to future business with other firms.

We are actually on the same page, but they fly off it when they try to exact a toll for the privilege or honor of working with them. It is true, as a rule, that companies have more power than you do and they want to use it to squeeze you.

You need to come back with a restatement of your value. This means you need to turn the tables. Pitch them on what a unique privilege it is to work with you. You are not a commodity like salt or sugar. It is not just your fingerprint that is unique. Your particular collection of attributes, your background, life experiences (or freshness if you are young and inexperienced), your education, prior training, all of these things are pertinent to supporting your perceived value.

Moreover, "How you disturb the molecules" when you are present or communicating remotely by phone and in writing is also incredibly important in making up the magical potion that is you. I heard this phrase when actor Glenn Close said about her co-actor, Jeremy Irons, "I like the way he disturbs the molecules when he enters a room." I always thought that was a nifty way of describing how chemistry changes when we interact.

Are there people you simply like being around? You want to come across to hiring authorities as that sort of individual. It is a highly paid quality. How can you do that? You can smile much more often than you frown. You can add some vocal variety to your voice. You can make and sustain friendly eye contact, reacting to others instead of constantly expressing your point of view. You can become a good listener. You can seem glad to be in the company of other people. The fact is that you and I have so many meaningful attributes other than the compensation we seek, that they are incalculable.

When companies are "Pulling a Tom Sawyer on you," hoping to get your services for free or for substantially less, they conveniently forget these other traits that are so important are making us mutually productive.

They say, "You are exactly like zillions of other work seekers and the only difference is price, so accept less." If you buy into this definition of your value you will never qualify for a high-paying job. There are occasions when we need to throw back the same arguments to those that are using them on us. "I'm sure you don't work for 50% of your actual value, so why would I?" See how they respond to that. Try saying, "I'm sorry, but I'm not an investment banker. I can't forego getting a fair wage in the hope of cashing in my equity for the big bucks later, can I?"

These retorts may get you thrown out on your ear, as they say. But even if they do, you will have asserted your value and preserved your self-respect. And you will be proud to hear yourself say, "I am worth a lot more and you will need to pay it to get my attention and services."

Don't be Tom Sawyered. If someone says you must pay them for the privilege of working, remind them that is not how good business works. They need to pay you and to pay you well.

Tip 29:
Learn From Machines, But Don't Toil Like One

I am astounded by the progress my children are making in their education. They are home-schooled, but that is really a misnomer. Mostly, they are Internet-schooled, and both of them are far ahead of where I was at their ages. They have already skipped grades!

Computers are great tools to learn from and through. But they are servants, and we need to remember this. One tipoff that we've gone astray is when we succumb to the inducements to work-as-machines-work. That is not where the money is so don't expect to be paid more than average or depressed wages if you are being hired to labor in a thoroughly repetitive manner. Let me give you an example.

As you may have surmised, among other skill sets I have developed very keen telephone communication capabilities. I teach inside sales skills and improve inside sales and customer services units in my consultancy. Part of my work is designing recruitment ads to attract capable sales candidates. I monitor ads to see what new wrinkles have been introduced and to see where the state of the art is at any given time. It never fails to surprise me when I see the following requirement: "Must be willing to make 100–300 calls per day!" If your computer is dialing, then it can sift through thousands of numbers in seconds. But that is not quite what the recruitment ad is saying. It is saying in so many words, "Expect to work like a robot!"

When dialing for sales, I know from vast experience that it is very difficult to get people to answer their lines if they don't recognize your phone number. Even if you're using "spoofed" numbers that appear to be in their same area code and locality, people typically do not answer calls. They let them go into voice mail, listen to the recordings, and then decide whether to phone back.

Therefore, many of these sales jobs are about continuously hunting for those that *will* answer their phones. Since there are so few in proportion to the numbers you must dial, you are making frightfully few actual, real-time contacts during the day. For business-to-business calls, you will likely reach one person per hour, on average. That fact has ripple effects. If you only speak to eight folks during a shift, I can tell you 6 of them will probably shut you down and dodge the conversation. "Call me back, later," they may say, and then when you do, they'll duck the call. If you're lucky you might have one or two "meaningful conversations" during the course of a shift. That is too few with which to sharpen your skills.

Why do baseball players take batting practice, even after they have reached the major leagues? It keeps them sharp. They *must* see lots of pitched balls to develop and retain what is called a "batter's eye." Getting back to my inside sales example, you won't sell well or sell enough people if you cannot have a good number of actual conversations.

In another section I mention a fellow that went for many months without a sale, and then earned a whopper of a commission on his first deal. That is unusual. But what is most significant for our purpose, now, is appreciating that his company put him in the position to make *a lot of money* when he had a meaningful conversation. Pitching two people a day was enough because the ultimate rewards were there. As we noted, he was paid more than $500 each and every hour, on average, to dial the phone, when we factor in the size of the bounty he was paid when he succeeded. That is super-rare. If a company is paying you to labor like a machine, to toil like a robot, to simply repeat a dumb routine, your wages will be depressed. They are admitting, tacitly, they have not devised a smarter way to succeed.

Successful businesses all endeavor to create what are called "rational routines." These are money-making procedures that predictably and reliably bring in profitable customers and keep them on the books. If your job is to perform these routines, in most cases, you will be paid poorly because the creative contribution you will be making will be minimal.

The more creativity and individuality and special handling that is required, the better your chances are of earning exceptional pay. Recently, I was speaking to a couple who works in professional ballet. She choreographs, directs, and teaches, and he performs around the world. At one point, knowing I am an author, she asked me, "Why don't you write a ballet?" Not needing any more encouragement, I took on the task and wrote a story. This is an ongoing project, so I can't tell you whether it will be wildly successful. But I can tell you there is a chance, if only because so few people today are writing and then producing and staging original ballets.

I have a chance to succeed at a high level of recognition and ultimately money because my creative contribution to the story is 100%. The only routine associated with its composition came from the fact that I am a disciplined scribe. I am used to writing something every day, so I have the confidence to try composing a work in a new medium. Apart from that, if I am paid for that work product it will be a result of the fact that writing ballets is not a widespread routine.

There is another way to screen jobs for their upside income potential. Ask yourself, are people having fun doing this? I mentioned professional baseball, which I know a little about. Are players at the major league level having fun? Typically, yes! They are being paid exceedingly well to play a kids' game.

Do TV news anchor people have fun? I have been a regular guest on several shows and I can tell you, up close and personal, they are having a blast. Do comedians have fun? Yes, and they have the most fun making other comedians laugh. I could go on and on. Generally, where there's fun there's money! Routines are fun-killers. I am not saying ballplayers, anchor people, and comedians don't work hard. They do, but it does not feel like work. And they have a huge amount of perceived control over how they get their jobs done. Autonomy, pleasure, originality, creativity are all elements associated with doing high-paying jobs.

If they are missing when you visit a potential employer, or if you detect it is violating some unwritten rule to deviate from strict norms, or to crack a smile or tell an occasional joke, you are in the wrong place. If you are not having fun you won't make money; at least, not for long!

Tip 30:
Create Multiple Streams of Income

When we think of creating a high-paying job, naturally our minds emphasize the idea of accomplishing this one job at a time. After all, the phrase says we are intending to develop "a" job instead of job(s). But we should challenge this assumption.

In another section we explore the idea doing two things at once, such as working full-time and going to school. I noted this can be symbiotic, one activity helping the other. I did it, and I found when one task had me down in the dumps, the other one picked me up. Seldom were both beating me up at the same time. A similar logic should be applied to creating high-paying work. Who says that your income must come from only once source at a time? Not me!

In fact, just yesterday I just got a few checks in the mail. One is from the University of California for a course I taught last month. The other is from publisher Simon & Schuster for a book of mine they published decades ago. Neither of these sources provides all that much revenue. But when we combine them with lots of royalty producing books and audios, corporate consulting, keynote speaking, individual career coaching, annuities, and other income streams I can put it this way. Tiny trickles can combine to produce raging rivers.

If I had to bundle all of my activities into one category, you could call me an "edu-preneur." I invent, develop, and market knowledge. This is important: If I had to rely only on one source, such as my seminars from universities, that income would not qualify as being "high," by my standards. Yet combined, these various sources become significant. And there are distinct advantages to seeking multiple streams of income, instead of one at a time. The old adage about not keeping all of your eggs in one basket comes to mind. Deriving all of your income from one source is a high-risk proposition. What if you are laid-off, or the company closes, or the organization loses funding? You are suddenly scrambling to find any opportunity that will keep your head above water. And when you are desperate we know that you are a terrible negotiator, unless you have ice water running in your veins. That means you could settle for a low-paying job, which is precisely the opposite of our aim for you. We're looking to move up, not down.

Same fact pattern, you lose that job. But in this case, your income derived from it is only a part of your overall inflow. You only need to find a small contribution from another source to restore you to your above-average cash flow. Comparatively, that's a lot easier to do than finding a 100% revenue substitute.

When I was a kid my first job was delivering newspapers. I worked for one of the two largest dailies in the Los Angeles area. But I was also ambitious. I wanted to earn more than I was being paid. Each day I was given a few extra papers that I could sell on a street corner or to passing traffic in the neighborhood. If I sold them, I pocketed the entire purchase price, which was a nice income boost. Still, it wasn't enough for me. So, I took on a second paper route, this one delivering for a local publication. It paid less than the major daily, but it was another income stream that helped me to earn far more than the typical newsboy. In theory, the second route was a natural because it took me through the exact, same neighborhood. Some households subscribed to both, so that was especially easy. By doubling routes I had the chance to double my tips around Christmas time. There was synergy. Though this is a modest example, I know, it is suggestive of a good way to do a little more and get far more for doing it.

I booked my university seminars around the country. To maximize the income I received, I organized these programs into tours. One day, I'd be in Louisville, and the next in Lexington, Kentucky and so forth. Knowing I would be in these spots, I booked myself on local talk radio shows to promote my books. Occasionally, I did a few days of corporate speaking along the way. I was able to make the most of my time and I was able to pass along travel savings to my sponsors. Each school and corporation was a unique income source. Alone, bringing me in to speak might have taken a larger budget and more approvals to obtain. Because I was "in the neighborhood," this fact got me more bookings plus it created a sense of urgency that got sponsors to make faster decisions about bringing me to their sites.

What if one university along the tour didn't "make?" Meaning, it failed to attract the required number of attendees to earn back its budget and it had to cancel. What, then? That meant I had an opening in the schedule that I could use to insert a substitute sponsor, or at worst, I would be able to take a breather and see the local sights. One lost date would not sink a tour or so substantially impact my overall revenue as to matter.

Once again, this is, the point. When you have multiple streams of income, the ones that persist will float your boat and carry you to where you need to go.

Just as conducting seminars in the four corners of our country and in Hawaii broadened me as a speaker, consultant, and person, when you divide your interests across a few income sources, you will learn more, as well. It is impossible to calculate the importance of this extra knowledge and savvy. None of it is lost; believe me.

Imagine a roulette table which has a lot of numbers. If you put all of your chips on one of those numbers, you can win big because the odds are against that one coming up. But if you spread your chips over two or more, the chance of one coming up in your favor, increases substantially.

I realize this runs contrary to the impulse to specialize, but I believe it makes more sense to keep your fingers in lots of pies. Also, it makes sense to diversify your income generating activities into short-term and long-term categories. Writing books and recording audios is all about the long-term. People discover my works across the years. This is to be expected. But you also need to generate short-term income. Some jobs combine a little of both. Salespeople in certain industries, such as insurance, are paid immediately when a client signs-up. They also get residual income each time the client makes a payment in the future. Does it appear that the insurance seller is making a ton of dough in his or her early years in the field? Not at all, but when you factor in the long term, insurance commissions resemble book royalties. No additional work needs to be done by the author or insurance seller, but the income continues.

There are lots of ways to earn a high income. Certainly, it can come from one job, but it might very well come from doing more than one, simultaneously.

Tip 31:
To Get What You Want, Know What You Want!

My wife and I were house hunting. We were about to settle for a floor plan that we had before. There was enough space for the family, but it was a case of "Been there, done that." I was not convinced this was the right place for us, and I sensed she wasn't completely sold, either. In a burst of clarity, I realized we might be making a major mistake, so I asked: "What do you *really* want?" She paused for a minute and replied, "Alex's house."

Alex's house was a different floor plan. It had dramatic ceilings and a spiraling staircase and three fireplaces. And it was on the water with a forty-foot boat dock. We love the water and we were leaving a house behind with a nice view of the breaking waves about two football fields away. Alex's house was a house that was once owned by, that's right, Alex. We thought of buying it, but passed.

Hearing her speak of Alex's house wistfully over the years, the abode that "got away," I knew exactly what was in her heart of hearts when I inquired about her real desire. "So, what are we doing here?" I asked. Promptly, we left the place we were standing in, deciding that though it was okay, it wasn't what we really wanted.

As it turned out, the original Alex's house came onto the market about two days later, and we grabbed it. Did it make her happy? It did! I'd say 95 percent of getting what you want is in *knowing* what you want. Five percent is figuring out how to put that Porsche in your driveway or that European vacation on your calendar. I was a not-so-happy college professor. I enjoyed so many aspects of that career that I still feel just a little guilty about saying it didn't completely fulfill me. I liked learning and doing research and preparing my lectures and class discussions. I also like to help people to grow, intellectually and professionally. The pace of an academic life was pleasing, coinciding with the flow of the seasons. Returning to school in autumn, wrapping it up in late spring, seemed to coincide nicely with rhythms deeply embedded in me. Occasional travel to professional conferences and conventions was fun. I loved public speaking, and still do.

There simply wasn't enough money in that career, and worse, because I was a tenure track assistant professor, I was staring down a thirty-year barrel of future penury. Would you go into a vocation that underpaid you for three decades, and then you could retire on an inadequate pension? Well, I was in it.

The question occurred to me: How can I do all of the enjoyable tasks of professor-ing without the poverty? That's what I *really* wanted. Moreover, I wanted to retain a connection to university life. To sum it up, I wanted to be a *very well paid professor*. That "job title" didn't exist. So, I had to create it.

I unbundled the tenure track assistant professor package. I took the preparation part along with original research aspect and devised a topic that I knew more about than any other college professor. It was telephone communication. Borrowing a phrase I learned later at Super Glue, one of my client's sites, I priced the seminar I developed "By the drop" and "Sold it by the gallon." Instead of working for universities by the quarter, semester, or year, I sold my seminars by the single day. They were one-day programs. Those were my droplets. By themselves, they paid me far less than I earned at a single university, teaching full-time. But collectively, those droplets turned into gallons inasmuch as I distributed my classes, widely.

Within 18 months of leaving my full-time post I was affiliated with 35 universities, a network I created, stretching from Hawaii to New York.

What I *really* wanted, yet wasn't completely conscious of, was more than money. I wanted *independence!* Instead of teaching courses that had already been titled, described, and taught before, I sought to invent my own, building them from scratch. I didn't want to sell a curriculum committee on endorsing my programs and then toiling to put content to them. Those courses would live on long after I was a memory at the university. I wanted to "own" those seminars. I didn't want to develop them and donate them to an institution that would get student funding from them and not share a nickel with me.

I had my dumb moment, and occasionally I still do. But when it comes to protecting my intellectual properties, I am vigilant. When I owned my subject matter it could be exclusive. It would take others some time before they could copy me. (And copy me, they did; later on!) In the meantime I could occupy the high competitive ground, setting and getting my prices and fees as I wished.

As I've said elsewhere, my customized seminars led to publishing half a dozen books in five years, establishing me as a best-selling author and prominent source of training and consulting. In a few years, I gained more notoriety in the form of media attention and newspaper, radio, and TV interviews than academics garner in a career, working as most do, in obscurity.

And I traveled like mad, learning about local nuances in my country and others, and that experience broadened me, tremendously. My granddad once gave my father some sterling career guidance. He said, "Use your *head*." I took this to mean being a "knowledge worker," as Peter F. Drucker would label those of us that labor with our minds.

Physical assets and money may come and go, as they are known to do during recessions and depressions. But your mind power, your intellectual abilities and properties can grow and grow. What do you *really* like and what elements of a job *must* you have to be happy? For me, it's intellectual and commercial independence. (If I knew you a little better I'd confess what I *really* like is making it up as I go along and not being told what to do.)

Write down what comes easily to you and what you like in a job or career. Next, eliminate those things that bother you about it. Ask, how can I get the benefits without bearing the burdens? If a job doesn't immediately come to mind, that's okay. You can make one up, as I did!

Tip 32:
Five Ways To Become Essential

I was tempted to title this section, "Five Ways to Become Indispensable." But no one is indispensable, as you may have heard. You could be relatively new to the workplace. If so, you haven't suffered through any severe recessions. I have, and I can say if a company is in a serious cost-cutting mode, nobody's job is safe. In their minds, managers and owners believe they can cut costs, endlessly as a means to hang on to dwindling profits or to keep their doors open. So, indispensability isn't our aim for you.

Being *essential* is something else. To me, being essential means you are needed. If you disappeared from the scene tomorrow, the company might not fall and not get up. But it would stumble and need to recover. One way to be essential is to do something no one else can do. Some folks become notaries to be the only one on staff that can vouchsafe documents. It doesn't take much training, but it is a certification and it can make you unique.

A second way to become essential is to over-deliver. This is very straightforward if you are in sales or in an area that is measured, objectively. Often, the top 10% of a sales team qualifies to become part of a President's Club. It may provide zero extra perks, but it is a recognition that you are one of the few doing the heavy lifting while carrying on your shoulders lesser performers. Keeping you aboard and even pampering you, becomes essential.

A third way to become essential is to help your boss to shine. I was doing a consulting assignment where there were two presidents of respective divisions. I worked for both, but one of them asked me if I felt the divisions could be merged or if they needed to remain separated. I realized what he was up to and that was taking over both units. I made him look good by saying, "There is no good reason they should remain separate," which was my assessment. I realized he would use my opinion to pitch himself to the CEO for more responsibility and better pay. He took over as chief of both divisions, and my consulting assignment was renewed.

A fourth way to become essential is to have an engaging personality and to have fun. I am not saying you should be the class clown, but if you can make an occasional joke, relieving tension at critical times, that contribution will be appreciated. Being easy to be around is a very positive trait and a great objective to take on. Part of that is not being openly critical, or constantly surfacing problems. If you spot an issue, choose to express it one-to-one with the right people. You will seem on the ball and your discretion will be appreciated. Being the first to get serious and to buckle down when there is a looming deadline is also an aspect of having a good workplace personality.

The fifth way to become essential is to be creative, to innovate. We just mentioned the idea of sharing problems with the right people. If you can follow your analysis with a suggestion or two for reducing or eliminating the problem, that goes far to enhance your credibility.

Problem-solvers are essential to every organization, much more than mere problem-spotters.

A way to bundle together these elements is to strive to become an internal consultant wherever you work. If someone's paperwork is always incomplete, causing backlogs and frustrations, you can offer to speak to the person. If the unit as a whole seems to be falling behind or becomes an obstruction you can offer to "go down there and see what's happening."

Even if you are turned down, the mere fact that you offered to go above and beyond your position description, to become a troubleshooter, is appreciated. I have taught this as a technique to be used in customer service staffs. As conversations conclude, I have reps ask if they can do more for the client or customer. Always without exception, the customer will say no, but they appreciate the offer.

I see this at my local supermarket, part of the Safeway chain. When I have only two or three items that are being bagged the clerk will ask, "Would you like help out to your car?" Thank goodness there is nothing about me physically that would suggest I need the assistance. And the small and light bag I'll be carrying certainly wouldn't require a cart or a person to assist. In fact, it is almost laughable that I would need help. Still, and please remember I *teach* this stuff, I appreciate the offer. Offering to your boss to do more, even if she or he is going to decline, still makes a hugely positive impression. You might say it puts emotional "coins" into your account. If you err, they will draw down a coin or two, cutting you some slack. If there are cutbacks in employment at your company, your savings account will tide you over while others are shown to the door.

Therefore, being essential means two over-arching things. (1) You are needed; and (2) You are wanted. I point to these because it is tempting to become pompous if we believe we are needed so much that we are indispensable. Pomposity and arrogance are typically punished. And those that emit these characteristics create the sort of animosity among their peers who cannot wait for them stumble and to see the end of them.

In other words, you can be super-competent, but unwanted. In the long run, that is a losing combination because folks will be trying to get rid of you, resenting the fact that they need you at all. And the obverse actually seems true, as well. If you are merely competent or even barely competent, yet you are wanted, your personality is super-rewarding; people will want to keep you around.

I had an accountant for more than two decades. We both entered business about the same time. He first did my taxes when I was 19, working for Time-Life. He had just received his college degree and was the most junior accountant on the staff of the firm. He went on to become a CPA and a partner and I formed my own very successful consulting practice. He had a great sense of humor and I liked him so much that I forgave his making some serious mistakes in judgment as the years passed. In one case, he could have saved me more than $25,000.00 in state taxes! But, his personality was so pleasant that I couldn't imagine doing taxes without him. Finally, we parted company, and overall I have no regrets.

The key to his longevity was that he became an essential part of my business routine, and it was easier to stick with him than to make a change. Don't shoot for indispensability. Instead do the five things I suggested to become essential and you'll create a high-paying job for yourself.

Tip 33:
Should You Work a Straight Commission Job?

In another section I mention the "millionaire salesperson" that went through a long, dry spell before earning his first sale and his first huge paycheck. That story, by itself says, potentially, there is a lot of money to be made by people willing to work on a contingency basis. Meaning, if they sell or perform in the requested way, they will prosper.

But should *you* work a straight commission job? I want to explore this question in detail, here. The answer could lead you to a lifetime of high-paying jobs. Also, quite obviously, it could enable you to have a good time while doing it. There are 10 things you should ask before accepting contingent pay, and specifically in a selling situation:

1. Ask, how long have you been in business? Beware of start-ups, because no one really knows whether their business concept will succeed. I realize what I am saying may seem counter-intuitive. After all, during the past few decades the rise of technology start-ups has become the stuff of legend and lore. Who wouldn't want to hitch their wagons to a rising star and get stock options that can be converted one day into zillions of bucks? Just today, I was offered a 50 percent share in a start-up. My role would be sup-

plying brainpower along with sales, marketing, and product development advice. Although I respect and like my would-be partner very much, I am exceedingly reluctant to jump aboard an under-funded ship that could sink at any time.

2. Ask, how much is your top salesperson earning? Divide the number by three or four and that's probably the most you'll earn during your first year. This is a great question, as are the ones that follow. But there is no answer that will be complete. For example, I was the number two seller at a company. I earned high pay and had a pretty good time while doing it. The very top seller had been there two years, since the inception of the company. I struggled to beat his performance, and by sharpening my approach and continuously improving, I came very close one month. At the very last minute, mysteriously, they "counted" a sale from who-knows-where, and he remained on the top perch. While I thought there was a level playing field, and he was beating me based on his merit, here's what was blurted out by the sales manager at a meeting. "That's why Tommy is given twice as many leads as anyone else!" All that time I thought it was a true competition, a meritocracy, but he was wired-into the system so much, that they pre-selected him as every contest winner. If you get twice as many leads you can get twice as many sales. This meant he was earning huge bonuses that were denied to the runner-up, me! So, back to my point: even if

they say the top seller is earning a huge amount and that is a fact, if they stack the deck against new hires, which happens a lot, that number you hear regarding his or her earnings should be put into proper perspective. The longer that top dog has been there, the greater the chances are that he is also wired into the system, the designated "favorite."

3. Ask, how long did it take for the top seller to earn that much? This is a vital cash-flow question. Can you survive until you start seeing regular paychecks? You may not have the time to go from A to B.

4. Ask, how long was it until your best seller made his first sale? Did she get lucky and close someone right away? Or, did she struggle? If the best seller struggled, multiply her time invested to the first sale by a factor of at least three or four, for yourself.

5. Ask about commission plan specifics: What percentage are they paying? Is there an appropriate incentive? Negotiate this to make it more appealing and sufficiently worthwhile to you. While we're on this point, let me mention something you'll see in employment ads. It is the phrase: "Uncapped Commissions!" There are some companies that do cap commissions. You may or may not realize if you have a modern car its software prevents you from reaching 200 miles per hour, or whatever your engine is naturally capable of reaching. Similarly, some compa-

nies say we will pay you commissions, but when you reach a certain level of earnings, your commissions will suddenly stop. IBM famously did this to Ross Perot. By the end of January, he met his quota of sales for not only that month, but also for the remaining 11 months in that year. There was absolutely no incentive for him to set foot into the office or the field on February 1. So, he quit IBM, started his own firm, and became a multi-billionaire; all because they capped his earnings. Some companies still do it, but the phrase "Uncapped Commissions!" is disingenuous. You may not earn enough to pay the rent in that job, but the phrase intimates that you'll certainly prosper. In other words, in most situations, it's a con. And that fact could be a good reason to avoid working for that company.

6. Ask, how well is your *worst* person doing? When they permit folks to struggle for weeks or months without substantial rewards that is a bad sign. There should be competition to earn a spot on their team, and the worst performers should be cut quickly. I don't want to sound cruel, but to me, there are very few occupational tortures than not achieving in a job, week after week and month after month.

7. Do you use a script? If they have a script and it is a proven success, this will save you a lot of time, presuming you follow it. If they allow no deviation from it, either they have selling down to a science

or they're needlessly strict. Especially if you're on a commission, they shouldn't care how you sell, as long as you sell, and you do it honestly. And of course, there are varying degrees of being scripted. A firm might require word-for-word compliance when you are just starting out and then relax the requirement later on. This isn't necessarily in your best interest, however. Sales slumps occur when successful sellers deviate from a winning routine. Upon returning to their scripts, quite often they see their sales reach or exceed prior, successful levels.

8. Are the hours flexible? If you are an independent contractor, this means you can come and go, or work remotely with some broad limitations. Some companies have a set start-time, and they want everyone to be there, for announcements, updates, and the like. But if they try to set the workday in concrete, unless they're paying for your time, they're overreaching. By doing this they deny you one of the upsides of being a commission seller, setting your own pace and being able to mix in other activities during the day.

9. At what intervals are commissions paid? This is significant. If they don't pay weekly, a flag should go up. You shouldn't be their bank, which is what you become with longer pay intervals. Intervals are negotiable. One of my coaching clients was looking for a sales gig while he built his part-time consulting practice. A firm offered him a draw of $4,000

against commissions. I told him to counter their offer with this statement, "Okay, I'll do $1,000 a week, payable weekly, okay?" Note, there are 4.333 weeks in a month. If he had been paid their way, he would have received $4,000.00 per month. My way, he received about $4,333.00. This is an extra guarantee of about $4000.00 per year. It is like adding a 13th month to an annual pay calendar. Plus, by insisting that we get checks weekly, he put the employer on a short financial leash. If it went belly-up, his exposure would only have been a week's worth of exertion.

10. Are there any reserves-against-commissions for charge-backs? When are they released? Charge-backs, or reductions in your commissions-paid, can occur when orders cancel or don't pay the company, as agreed. Sometimes, firms try to protect themselves against paying a commission for a deal that falls through. Accordingly, they may hold back 10–15% of your check. Ask them, when are these funds released to you, and if you leave the job will they still pay you your reserves and unpaid commissions?

Let me emphasize these elements are negotiable!

It is quite typical for small companies, especially, to have a different pay plan in place for each seller. So, if they say, we can give you a draw against commissions, but it will only be minimum wage, two things should enter your mind. I can improve this through some dickering, and something guaranteed, however small, is better than nothing. Let me speak to this last point. When companies are entrenched in the belief that they shouldn't have to pay any kind of guarantee, it makes me a little suspicious. First and foremost, they are shifting the risk of failure to the worker. If they know what they are doing, they should be able to train a new person quickly and make that person productive in record time.

"The math of success" should be so well known that upon request they can recite it to you. They might say: "You should earn your first commission within X days. After that the minimum we should see from you are Y sales, and we expect you to be at that level within a month. If you are, you'll be earning Z dollars. If they dodge the question, saying, "Well it varies so much from person to person," a flag should go up. You're speaking to someone deceptive or to a bozo that does not have any clue as to what is truly going on.

Solid companies are not afraid to permit you to do a ride-along, of sorts where you are paired with a successful seller for a day or more. You can observe her in action and she can informally train you. When you hear and see her succeeding, you have a degree of proof that their methods are working, and this is more than reassuring. It is vital to have confidence in them. Any insecurity that you have about your employer will be communicated inadvertently and unconsciously to your prospects. If you are not completely sold on your firm, they won't be, either.

A commission sales job, or contingent pay can be a fantastic opportunity. It offers the prospect of high rewards with flexible hours, and it is perhaps the closest you can come to being in your own business without a lot of the hassles. But be sure to ask these ten questions before leaping into the fray. It could make the difference between earning and missing some serious pay!

Tip 34:
Ask For What You Want!

There is a crucial difference in how men and women negotiate, according to Harvard research, as well as anecdotal evidence. Women *ask less often* than men.

First, they are more apt to think they cannot negotiate in many situations where men think they can. And then, women simply fail to let the words come out of their mouths, words that when heard could elicit a yes response. The Bible offers the famous passage in the Book of Matthew that I'll paraphrase: Ask and you will receive; Knock and it will be opened to you; Seek and you will find.

We know many things about negotiating for bigger and better pay at work and for getting more desirable perks. The more frequently you ask, the better the chance you have of hearing a yes. The more you ask for, i.e. the bigger the salary or the raise you are requesting, the more money you will be granted. The more people you ask, the greater your odds of hearing yeses, in general.

In my book, *The Law of Large Numbers: How to Make Success Inevitable*, I say: Do enough of anything and you will succeed. Do more than that, and you'll probably prosper and grown rich. Outdo even that amount of activity, and you could become a legend.

The book *Rejection Proof*, by Jia Jiang echoes this theme. He invented running shoes that had little wheels in them, making them like skateboards without the boards. You've seen them, I'm sure. They became a big hit, but not for Jiang. You see, he had his patentable drawings locked in a drawer, too shy to take his invention to the next level. In the meantime, another inventor, two years later, came up with the same plan but he patented his and became rich.

Jiang determined that he was deficient in one area: He was too sensitive to rejection. So, he set forth to conquer this fear. He did it by purposely seeking rejections for 100 days in a row. His first rejection came when he asked a total stranger, a security guard, if the fellow would lend him $100. He went into a pet-grooming salon and asked if they would cut his hair.

The list goes on. What he found is even with absurd requests like asking a homeowner if he could play soccer in his backyard, some folks would try to say yes. When asked why he agreed to let Jiang play ball there, the guy said Jiang's request was so off the wall, "How could I say no?" The point is that *asking* is essential to creating a high-paying job for oneself. We know from the practice of negotiation around the world this simple fact: If you don't ask, you won't get what you want. Typically, people will not hound you to accept bundles of dough, even if you deserve it. You must make yourself worthy, and a threshold requirement is to be willing to ask, and then to do it.

I was doing a major customer service training program in Texas. It took months to train everyone in my methods. And then the time came to go operational. My contact, the Senior Vice President of Customer Service asked me, "Why aren't they using it?" referring to the conversational path I invented and trained them to use? I slowly replied, "They are waiting for you to say they *must* do it, to *ask* them to do it, *now*." A second later, she started walking among the cubicles, saying "Okay, let's use the call path!" and they did. The program succeeded wildly. The unit rose to the top of its industry in customer satisfaction ratings. An even bigger company bought them out, for big bucks, and my methods staying in place for a dozen years, as did their top service award receipts.

It is all about *asking* people to do that which they had been trained to do. It is a matter of inertia, which is one of the iron laws of thermodynamics. A body at rest tends to stay at rest, unless it is nudged. A request is a nudge. Without it, there is no movement. I mentioned earlier that the more you ask for the more you will get. This is a very important precept.

People perennially make a fundamental negotiation mistake. For demonstration, I am going to use an arbitrary number, $100. Let's say you have added up your living expenses, thrown in a little extra for fun, and the figure you arrive at is $100. Now you are negotiating salaries with employers. What are you likely to do? You will probably ask them to pay you $100. Here's what happens. You will be negotiating with someone that is used to going back and forth, hearing an offer, countering that offer, haring a compromise, and then responding to that.

Unless you have so underpriced your labor, these savvier folks will *never* accept the first offer, because they have been trained not to. They may come back with $80. Eighty-dollars? "I can't live on that!" you're thinking. You reply, "But I need a hundred." They say, "Well, maybe we can go to 85."

You're insistent, because math is math and you know you need $100 to pay for essentials and to have a tiny bit left over for goodies or emergencies. But you are deadlocked on the $100 number because you have given yourself no negotiation room. You may end up accepting $85 because you'll throw out the frills, but that's no way to live.

You should have aimed higher, asking for at least 20% more that you actually needed. That means you should have started around $125 or $120. Then, they could have come up $20 and you could have come down by $20, and voila! You'd both be happy right in the middle at $100, which was your target. The key here is to ask for more and you will get more. It is crucial in creating a high paying job.

The third precept I mentioned is to ask around widely, asking a lot of different people. I did a nationwide consulting project for Xerox Computer Services. One of their sales managers was very sharp. He explained his #1 selling principle. He called it, "Get in and spread out." Let's say he would have a meeting with the head of Information Technology. While he was there he'd ask if the IT person would be kind enough to introduce him to the Chief Operations Officer. In this way he made more effective use of his time and he spread his influence over more contacts. Each person he met became another possible budget he could tap to sell his computer services.

Companies are porous. There are several points of entry. Just because one door may be closed to you doesn't mean all doors will be closed. Human Resources may toss away your resume, but the office of the President may receive it and pass it to the right operational person in your area of interest.

Lots of people can "create" jobs for you, but they need to know you exist and what you want. Again, that means you need to ask more often, ask for more money, and ask more widely.

Tip 35:
Get Mad And Get Rich

I was consulting for a Midwest-based company in the gift packaging industry. This was a successful firm run by a naturalized citizen. He bought the business five or six years before and was interested in refining its inside sales function. Having read one of my bestselling books on the topic he was confident I could help him reach his ambitious goals.

One thing I noticed and commented on was his autocratic management style. I suggested lightening-up. Instead of using a top-down method of giving orders he should empower workers to govern themselves and take responsibility. Offended by this suggestion, he explained: "What you're saying is exactly what I ran away from in my old country, a communal consciousness. That doesn't work for me!"

In other words, he was happy the way he was and found nothing wrong with his heavy-handed approach. To him, the best antidote to worker indifference and underachievement was a continuous kick in the butt. To take this a little farther, not only did he perceive his authoritarianism as a non-problem, he attributed his ongoing success exactly to that method of command and control.

This flew in the face of nearly everything that I was taught in management school. There, the idea of his "Theory X" style was like the work of the devil. Long ago, it was pushed to the side by "Theory Y," a more humanistic and enlightened manner of dealing with workers.

Indeed, the very terms I'm using, "Workers" instead of the more contemporary and accepted term, "Associates," tells the tale of how we have moved away from industrial dictatorship to something resembling egalitarianism. And yet, the pesky fact remains. There isn't just one style that works to get things done.

Steve Jobs was famous for his authoritarianism and his perfectionism. Much of Apple's success is traced to his demanding style and insistence on controlling every part of the process of bringing new products to market.

One of the benefits of being in the labor market for several decades is that it gives you a long perspective. Today, I see management theories as haute couture. They really belong in the fashion industry. Meaning, they come and go. For a while they determine what everyone should be wearing, and then other styles replace the former ones. Like hemlines, they rise and fall with the years, only to rise again. Companies purchase "fad" methods from Consultant A and then swiftly toss them away in favor of the opposite methods from Consultant B. And then, over time, they may revert to Consultant A's approach.

When it comes to developing your career and creating high-paying jobs for yourself, I recommend you operate like that client of mine did, in the gift business. Specifically, I suggest using what one of my early speech teachers advocated using to build stunning presentations: Righteous Indignation. This translates into seeing a wrong, feeling its injustice deeply, and then righting it. In other words, don't be indifferent about a job. Love it or hate it. If you cannot do either of these things, then leave it.

Today, there is a word that you'll see in employment ads: "Passion." It tries to tap into what I'm saying, but it doesn't do it well. Companies say, especially in their lofty mission statements, "We're passionate about serving customers." In truth, they are far more passionate about serving shareholders and themselves. That is not what I mean when I suggest using the rocket fuel that is in righteous indignation.

To create a significantly above average opportunity you need to be *angry* about your current circumstances. You must be committed to improvement, *now*. My brother, a keen observer of human nature, told me when I was in my late teens and about to become fully self-supporting: "Gary, people don't get anything done until they get *disgusted* with the way things are."

We need to see there is a gap between the way things are and the way they need to be. Right now, in your mind, there may be no gap. You might have a job that pays the bills, provides some insurance, and possibly contributes a little to a retirement account. It's comfortably routine.

I spoke to a fellow two days ago who works in exactly this atmosphere, for a municipality. He counts the days to retirement when he can spend more time with his family and do the kinds of breezy things he did in his youth. He realizes he is making a sacrifice for his family.

And yet, he would not be a candidate to create a high-paying job for himself. And why is this? He would have to admit there is a current gap in what he wants and what he needs. He would have to let that disturbing notion well up in him, that feeling of a shortfall, a loss. You might be in clover, but you cannot let that little patch of comfort be good enough.

There are a lot of New Yorkers that move to Los Angeles. While they do well, professionally, many of them share the same fear. That is, the easy life, great weather, and lack of adversity will soften them. Then they will lose the success they have achieved. Some move back East because of this concern. They know they work best and achieve the most when their limits are tested and enlarged.

I am saying you need to be aware of your own Complacency Factor. Are you feeling numb most of the time, unmotivated to achieve anything great? Then you need to set higher goals, now. By doing this, you will create the gap I am speaking of between how things are and how they should and *must* be.

My Brooklyn-born brother-in-law said some years ago, "Gary we're a lot like each other. We're both afraid to be poor and this is what motivates us." He was right, and I toiled obsessively to become affluent, to make money irrelevant.

You will create and accept the type of job that is consistent with your goals and your discomfort with the distance you are from those goals. Don't rationalize that it is okay to allow that gap to exist without exerting supreme efforts to close it. Don't succumb to the money myths that losers recite, such as "Money is the root of all evil," and "Money can't make you happy," and "Money is dirty, and I'm above wanting it." Feel the pain of watching others get what you want and don't have. Get *mad* about that, feeling righteously indignant.

What I am saying is the exact opposite of calmly accepting the ways things are and detaching yourself from the pain. This is not about embracing Zen. It is exactly the anti-Zen.

Doris Drucker, Peter's spouse, a scientist in her own right, studied the highest achieving Chief Executive Officers in corporations. In a speech she gave at Claremont Graduate University's Peter. F. Drucker School of Management, she pointed out that there were some notable shared characteristics among those top CEO's. They were not exemplars of peace and tranquility, having reached the top rungs of management and the pinnacles of pay. They were constantly unsatisfied, and many of them led less than fulfilling family lives. I know, this is a pretty stark observation, but it rang true when I heard her say it, and it rings true today.

You will need to pay a price to create a high-paying job. Stir yourself up, get mad, and then get rich!

Tip 36:
Want More Pay? Guarantee You'll Be Worth It

I was descending the outside stairs at our home in the forest when my wife, who was below, spotted a rattle-snake. She warned me at the last second. Instead of allowing my foot to accidentally touch it I elevated my knee and stomped it to death. That was the new reflex that I had drilled after eight years of intensive karate lessons, culminating in a black belt. The human fear of snakes is bred into us. This has great survival value.

The human fear of losing money is acculturated into managers, bosses, and business owners. Why don't they spontaneously offer us great pay and develop special jobs for us to do, simply as a matter of course? They are afraid they won't get an adequate return on their investments. They fear they will lose money, time, and they will suffer potential embarrassment. These concerns seem insurmountable, don't they? But they aren't.

Their worries imply a solution. If we can guarantee them they will not lose, and that the goal we are pursuing is meritorious and within reach, their objections to granting our wishes should fall away.

There are two types of guarantees: Subjective and Objective. Here is the first sort: "If at any time you think I'm not pulling my weight or more than paying you back your investment in me, then just say so, and we'll part company." That is subjective because it is based merely on the other person's perception. I have said, "If at any time you don't think . . ."

I could have said, "If at any time you don't feel . . ." and it would work the same way. They don't have to prove anything. They simply need to assert the deal isn't working out.

An Objective Guarantee comes with strings attached. I sold many customer service improvement programs by stating I would reduce average talk times on the phone by 20 percent or more. We would start with a pilot program, training 10 percent or 20 percent of their people. If they showed the predicted improvement in abbreviating conversations, I would be permitted to complete the program, training 100 percent of the staff.

I had already established the dollar savings associated with succeeding in abbreviating calls. If it was $2 million in the first year, I could easily cost-justify being paid $500,000.00 to accomplish this task. They would pocket $1.5 million in first year savings, and the same or more in the years that followed.

There is "proportionality" to what you can earn, to what people will perceive as "fair pay." This isn't scientific; it is largely intuitive. Same example as above, but what if I said I needed to split the savings and be paid a million dollars? I would have encountered resistance, perhaps not universally.

But if I could show they were getting three slices of a pie and I was only getting one, it seemed to arouse their greed reflexes. I felt I saved marketing time by charging less. To elaborate on this point, briefly let me share an exercise I do with my negotiation trainees.

I say to them: "Given your current circumstances, let's say I came to you with this offer. I want you to join me in a deal where I will be paid $10 million and you will receive $1 million. What do you think? Is that attractive to you?" What would you say to that? Would you like it? Would you feel there's something wrong with my offer? Might you be offended? My trainees mostly react this way: "That's not FAIR!" they exclaim. "So, you wouldn't take the deal?" I reply. "No way!" most concur.

The rare person might sense there is something askew in the common reflexive reactions expressed by listeners. Most are, indeed offended, feeling that they are being taken advantage of.

I set a trap. I said, "Given your current circumstances, let's say I came to you with this offer . . ." Most of my trainees are not independently wealthy or paid millions for their ministrations. I came to them offering *them* one million dollars. Therefore, they will walk away with one million more dollars than they currently have. What's wrong with that offer? In absolute terms, it is an unusually agreeable deal, to be paid a million bucks. But in relative terms, it seems woefully deficient because I am getting nine million *more* dollars than you are.

What if my contribution to the deal is ten thousand times more than yours? If I'm only getting nine or ten times more, then it is you that is getting a steal of a deal, correct? Perceived unfairness will kill deals, even if they should be attractive to all participants. Thus, when

I speak of "proportionality," how much you get in light of how much I get, there are highly emotional reflexes that enter decision making. Strict rationality flies out the window.

Another way of saying this is to point out that employers or business partners should not count your money. Instead, they should count *theirs*. That would be the rational way of assessing what is desirable. As long as they are coming out ahead of where they started, they should embrace their earnings and be satisfied.

I know a consultant that worked for the Yellow Pages directories, which ran paid advertisements. He noticed that companies designed their ads in sub-optimal ways. They bought too much space, didn't use color or symbols appropriately, and in effect, they were overpaying for the business they received from the exposure.

He decided to launch a consulting business for the specific purpose of saving these companies money when they purchased Yellow pages ads. Typically, they could buy less space, save big, and pay him 20 percent of the savings he achieved on their behalf. Thus, he created a high paying job for himself. He netted far more as a consultant than he did as a Yellow pages seller.

He came to me because he wanted to raise the percentage he charged for his service. He also wanted to be paid for longer than one or two Yellow pages billing cycles. This is pretty much the same situation as I was in when I promised to abbreviate calls. I knew what my clients didn't know about shortening conversations while making them better.

They were willing to pay me to train them to do it, but they resisted paying licensing fees to continue to use my methods in the future. (Still, I convinced most of them to pay these, as well.)

But there is resentment when you inaugurate a new way to be paid. At some point, by charging certain percentages or by seeking to prolong the time people pay, you will evoke resistance, resentment, and non-agreement.

What I do know is this: If you say, "What difference does it make *how much* you pay me? You are still saving money you would never save without me!" this doesn't have the persuasive impact you might expect.

At certain levels of pay, forces will be unleashed in companies to get rid of you. If for no other reason, they will say it isn't "fair" for you to earn extraordinary money while the rank and file in ordinary posts earn so much less. Or, they will imitate you and try to figure out how to do things all on their own.

Expect this. It is part of being outstanding, standing out, and making an exceptional contribution to success. To get the chance to be pushed out for earning too much, gain admittance in the first place by guaranteeing your results.

Tip 37:
Get A Mentor And Become One

It was a chilly but beautiful late autumn in London. On an extended stay, I was making a point of catching the theater season. I wasn't disappointed. I saw Maggie Smith, Edward Fox, Albert Finney, Paul Scofield, Jeremy Brett, and other luminaries perform.

On my way to the city of Bath, I stood in the train station, hands empty, with nothing to do but wait. I always try to have a book or my clipboard and writing tablet, and this time I felt naked without them. Spotting a book kiosk, I scanned the titles. The name Drucker leapt out at me. A small but chunky abridgment of Peter F. Drucker's most famous work on management was soon in my hands, and I didn't put it down during my entire commute.

Instantly, I experienced what millions of others had before me. It was a sense of déjà vu. I had seen Drucker's ideas in action as a corporate manager, a longtime consultant, an entrepreneur, educator, and as a trainer.

One passage alone, about "The Fallacy of Creativity," electrified me. I had recently lived just what he was talking about. Indeed, the problem he identified was something I faced almost daily as a corporate consultant in getting people to try my new ideas.

The Fallacy of Creativity

There is a centuries-old and continually revived slogan of the individual's creativity: 'Free people from restraint and they will come up with far better, far more advanced, far more productive answers than the experts.'

But there is no evidence to support this belief. Everything we know indicates that creativity can become effective only if the basic tools are given.

Everything we also know indicates that the proper structure of work—of any work—is not intuitively obvious.

People have shoveled sand for untold centuries. Most of the time, one can assume, nobody told them how to do it. If making work productive depended upon the creativity of people, they would undoubtedly have found the best way of doing the job before the dawn of history.

Yet when Taylor first looked at the job in 1885, he found everything was wrong.

The amount of sand the shoveler lifted in one operation was the wrong amount, was indeed the amount most calculated to tire him and to do him physical harm. The containers were the wrong shape, the wrong size, and in the wrong position, and so on.

Human intuition and creativity had produced an operation that was both backbreaking and inefficient.

The process was improved by several orders of magnitude by being analyzed and then synthesized again into a single productive operation.

> *And exactly the same total mis-design of work and process after two thousand years of 'creativity' was found when physicians first systematically analyzed the process of medical diagnosis.*

Drucker, Peter F. *Management*. London: Pan Books, 1979. Print.

I reproduced this passage because over the course of a few pages Drucker was able to rebut most of the corporate "empowerment" movement that was sweeping organizations.

That craze operated from the opposite premise: That the people closest to the work should be the work's designers. Their everyday wisdom was supposedly more likely to create breakthroughs in processes than the experts could ever devise. But I knew a different reality.

In my reality, those closest to the work felt the way they were doing it was superior to any possible alternative. They could be shown a better way to shovel sand and they would reject it simply because they didn't invent it. They preferred bad habits to new habits. If you tried to replace their shovels, they'd beat you over the head with them.

In other words, workers closest to the problem were part of the problem, and typically, they refused to detach themselves from it.

Soon after reading this segment, I incorporated Drucker's thinking into my corporate classes. I actually discussed the "Fallacy" with the very people that were resisting my ideas, and with their managers.

It helped to start a meta-communication, a higher-level conversation about promoting change and allowing results only, to determine best practices.

At the end of that book there was a brief notation that Drucker was a professor at Claremont Graduate University, in Claremont, California. That was about 55 miles from where I lived and headquartered my consultancy. "I wonder if he's still teaching."

I phoned the school and found he was teaching in the MBA program at the Peter F. Drucker Graduate School of Management, named in his honor. I explained to the staffer that I had a Ph.D. and a law degree, and I also taught at the college level. "Could I take a class with him?"

Well, I did more than that. I signed up for a certificate program and later for an Advanced Executive MBA degree, taking most of my courses with Drucker. And I became his informal chauffeur on Saturday afternoons, when he taught most of his classes. We spent a lot of time talking about his ideas, and mine. Graciously, he even shared some of his consulting clients.

Drucker was a mentor to me. He had a profound influence on my thinking and on my career. So, in part, this program is about him and his ideas. I'll highlight what I think are some of his greatest concepts.

But there is an even broader and more influential topic underneath. And that is the art and science of *mentoring*. By mentoring, I mean working one-on-one with another person for the purpose of mutual enhancement and enlightenment. In the material that follows, I am going to discuss the importance of finding, studying with, and working with mentors. You will learn how to contact them, have them accept you as a mentee, and how to get the greatest benefit from them. You will also learn those skills necessary to become a first-class mentor.

I believe we learn more, we learn faster, we learn more deeply, and more meaningfully when we interact with the best people in their fields.

I mentioned earlier about reading an interview with actor Glenn Close. She was speaking about Jeremy Irons, her co-star in the Broadway production of "The Real Thing." She said, "I like the way he disturbs the molecules when he enters the room." That notion of "disturbing the molecules" is a great way of saying Irons has charisma or great chemistry or good vibes.

Something akin to this "disturbance" occurs in the presence of the best mentors. You are affected by their presence. I feel the need to "Bring my A-game" and to "Step-up" when I'm dealing with these great resources. They are the best, so I need to be at my best. I earn the privilege of sharing that common space, and re-earn it each time we meet.

Drucker is but one of the "great minds" and "great doers" I have affiliated with. I have worked with many others, from entrepreneurs to martial arts gurus, identifying what it is, specifically, that makes these masters so effective and so influential.

The expression, "A word to the wise is sufficient," is only part of the story. In reality, "A word *from* the wise," is even more important. A source's credibility and gravitas are crucial in their impact on the learning experience and on our growth and development.

Mentors have made history and have written it. Plato mentored Aristotle, and Aristotle mentored Alexander the Great. And today, because of the Internet, mentoring is becoming possible and is being reinvented on a scale not seen for hundreds of years.

There is a massive movement underway in primary and secondary education: Home schooling. Millions of parents are staying home with their kids, working one on one with them, to improve the quality of education they receive. This is being co-facilitated by online instruction with credentialed teachers. My girls, this minute, are achieving at levels far above their age-delineated grade levels. It is astonishing to see how vastly superior the learning process is when it is scaled back to a one-to-one format.

Another contemporary face of mentoring is found in "coaching." People are seeking out career coaches, life coaches, relationship coaches, and others that can help them with a miscellany of problems and opportunities. Mentoring differs from coaching in many cases because coaches don't have the credentials, experience, and track records that great mentors typically have. Still, I believe the one-to-one format of engagement is so powerful that great results can be obtained even when coaches don't meet the same standards as mentors.

I am reminded of the story that took place in San Francisco, near Fisherman's Wharf. Someone rented a tiny storefront and hung a banner in the window that read: Professional Listener: Reasonable Rates.

Apparently, all the person did was listen to others that gladly paid them by the half hour for the chance to be heard. Word has it that the business thrived. My point is that being paid attention to, actually engaging with another person one to one, is so agreeable that people will pay for it and find great benefit in the encounter.

Even without the advice that is essential in our conception of mentoring, being heard, and better yet, being listened to and perhaps understood on one's own terms, is very agreeable. It humanizes us. It makes us feel, at least for that half-hour, that we are worth focusing on, that our needs come first in someone else's life.

I am a professional mentor. I have taught at the college level for decades, and of course I have counseled my students one to one. I have done the same for corporate executives as a professional consultant, and I offer one-to-one coaching to some of my readers, listeners, and seminar trainees. So, I have a major stake in this topic.

Actually, we all do. In a world where we can feel insignificant, where we are competing with billions of others for our daily bread, being shown personally how to cope, how to bring out our best, and how to provide for ourselves and our families is a tremendous, and I believe, essential opportunity. It is one that we cannot afford to pass up.

I have five earned college degrees: BA, MA, PhD, JD, and MBA. But how impressive are they compared to this statement: "I studied, personally, with Peter F. Drucker for two-and-one-half years"?

You have the same opportunity, though not with Drucker, who has passed on. But you can work with me, time permitting. You can create a unique pedigree for yourself, one that will open doors, and say more than any degree can say.

Plus, you will learn in ways that are not available en masse, through a book, taking an online course, or even sitting in yet another generic course. If you are a mentor, or aspire to become one, this is a great, highly paying career in itself.

They say, "A teacher never knows where his influence stops." Ditto for great mentors. Find one or become one, now!

Afterword

Thank you very much for reading *How to Create Your Own High-Paying Job*. I hope the tips, examples, stories, and other materials will inspire you and help you to achieve much more in your career and in your life.

Throughout, I've mentioned some of my other books, audios, seminars, and related offerings. I just want to point out that they exist and are also available to you through the typical channels. An Amazon or Google search will uncover many of these titles.

I also invite you to contact me directly with your questions and comments. I mentioned I am available as a mentor and a consultant on a limited basis, if you feel you would benefit from one-to-one assistance.

I am going to list a few of my current email addresses below with the understanding that they may change from time to time.

(818) 970-4279

gary@customersatisfaction.com

gary@negotiationschool.com

drgaryscottgoodman@yahoo.com

gary@drgarygoodman.com

Hope to hear from you, and all my best to you!

—Dr. Gary S. Goodman